Britta Hummel

Description Logic for Scene Understanding

Britta Hummel

Description Logic for Scene Understanding

at the Example of Urban Road Intersections

Südwestdeutscher Verlag für Hochschulschriften

Impressum/Imprint (nur für Deutschland/ only for Germany)
Bibliografische Information der Deutschen Nationalbibliothek: Die Deutsche Nationalbibliothek verzeichnet diese Publikation in der Deutschen Nationalbibliografie; detaillierte bibliografische Daten sind im Internet über http://dnb.d-nb.de abrufbar.

Alle in diesem Buch genannten Marken und Produktnamen unterliegen warenzeichen-, marken- oder patentrechtlichem Schutz bzw. sind Warenzeichen oder eingetragene Warenzeichen der jeweiligen Inhaber. Die Wiedergabe von Marken, Produktnamen, Gebrauchsnamen, Handelsnamen, Warenbezeichnungen u.s.w. in diesem Werk berechtigt auch ohne besondere Kennzeichnung nicht zu der Annahme, dass solche Namen im Sinne der Warenzeichen- und Markenschutzgesetzgebung als frei zu betrachten wären und daher von jedermann benutzt werden dürften.

Verlag: Südwestdeutscher Verlag für Hochschulschriften Aktiengesellschaft & Co. KG
Dudweiler Landstr. 99, 66123 Saarbrücken, Deutschland
Telefon +49 681 37 20 271-1, Telefax +49 681 37 20 271-0
Email: info@svh-verlag.de
Zugl.: Karlsruhe, Universität Karlsruhe (TH), Dissertation, 2009

Herstellung in Deutschland:
Schaltungsdienst Lange o.H.G., Berlin
Books on Demand GmbH, Norderstedt
Reha GmbH, Saarbrücken
Amazon Distribution GmbH, Leipzig
ISBN: 978-3-8381-1423-1

Imprint (only for USA, GB)
Bibliographic information published by the Deutsche Nationalbibliothek: The Deutsche Nationalbibliothek lists this publication in the Deutsche Nationalbibliografie; detailed bibliographic data are available in the Internet at http://dnb.d-nb.de.

Any brand names and product names mentioned in this book are subject to trademark, brand or patent protection and are trademarks or registered trademarks of their respective holders. The use of brand names, product names, common names, trade names, product descriptions etc. even without a particular marking in this works is in no way to be construed to mean that such names may be regarded as unrestricted in respect of trademark and brand protection legislation and could thus be used by anyone.

Publisher: Südwestdeutscher Verlag für Hochschulschriften Aktiengesellschaft & Co. KG
Dudweiler Landstr. 99, 66123 Saarbrücken, Germany
Phone +49 681 37 20 271-1, Fax +49 681 37 20 271-0
Email: info@svh-verlag.de

Printed in the U.S.A.
Printed in the U.K. by (see last page)
ISBN: 978-3-8381-1423-1

Copyright © 2010 by the author and Südwestdeutscher Verlag für Hochschulschriften Aktiengesellschaft & Co. KG and licensors
All rights reserved. Saarbrücken 2010

Acknowledgements

Meinem Doktorvater Prof. Stiller möchte ich dafür danken, dass ich viel von ihm lernen durfte und dass er mir viel ermöglicht hat –vom Industrieprojekt mit der Firma Bosch über unsere Teilnahme am Grand Challenge bis zu meinen Auslandsaufenthalten in Australien und den USA. Vielen Dank!

Bei Prof. Möller bedanke ich mich für die Übernahme des Koreferats, die Einladung nach Hamburg und den Besuch in Karlsruhe, und ganz besonders für den stets angenehmen, konstruktiven und motivierenden Austausch! Besonderer Dank gebührt Michael Wessel, der unermüdlich Rede und Antwort stand zu allen Fragestellungen rund um RACER.

Ein weiteres Dankeschön gilt meinen Studienarbeitern, Diplomanden und Hiwis. Zongru, Werner, Laura, Michael, Jürgen –ich habe die Arbeit mit Euch als Bereicherung erlebt.

Meiner Mutter danke ich, dass sie mein Interesse für Technik von kleinauf unterstützt hat, und meinem Vater postum dafür dass er mir ein finanziell weitestgehend sorgenfreies Studium ermöglicht hat.

Asarnusch, Dominik, Hans-Peter, Holger, Katrin und Werner, Ihr wart und seid die weltbeste Studiclique!

Irina, Bianca und Tina, danke für den moralischen Beistand während schwieriger Zeiten.

Abschließend bedanke ich mich bei der Deutschen Forschungsgesellschaft, die diese Arbeit im Rahmen des Sonderforschungsbereich/Transregio 28 finanziell gefördert hat.

Britta Silke Hummel

II

Abstract

Understanding a natural scene on the basis of external sensors is a task yet to be solved by computer algorithms. Solving it for non-microworlds requires an appropriate formalism for representing and reasoning with sensor data and domain knowledge. The present thesis investigates the suitability of a particular family of explicit, formal languages for this task, which are subsumed under the term Description Logic (DL). DL is an offspring of First Order Logic, inheriting a well-defined, declarative semantics, but offering improved computational tractability and an object-oriented knowledge engineering paradigm.

The first part of this contribution elaborates on principled approaches for representing scene information, and for solving Scene Understanding tasks, in the DL formalism. For several typical classes of information, generic DL representations are proposed in the form of design patterns. In particular, for axiomatising data from an external sensor, representations are developed for a redundant vs. complementary sensor set, and for partial vs. locally complete data. For axiomatisation the hypothesis space of admissible scene geometries with respect to a given domain, a graphical specification along with its DL translation is developed. Several classic mid-level problems from the Computer Vision domain are shown to be solvable using deductive DL reasoning. These tasks are namely collective object classification, object detection, and data association.

The second part describes an extensive case study in the application domain of road intersections. It introduces the ROad Network oNtologY RONNY, a DL ontology which models the qualitative geometry and building regulations of roads and intersections for the purpose of Scene Understanding, making extensive use of the proposed patterns. RONNY's task-solving performance is evaluated on a set of complex, natural intersection scenes, using as input data an experimental vehicle's stereo vision system, a digital map, and a global positioning system. The following tasks are posed to the system for each intersection: Object classification ("Which driving directions are permitted on each lane?", "What traffic participants are allowed on each lane?"), object detection ("Between which lane pairs do driveable paths exist?"), and data association of multiply detected lanes ("Which of the map's lanes is equivalent to the vehicle's ego lane?").

The results provide qualitative and quantitative support in favour of the argument, that a logic-enhanced system significantly improves recognition rates of state-of-the-art quantitative Computer Vision, and enables to tackle more complex tasks that are beyond the current scope. The contribution concludes with an evaluation of the deductive DL formalism with respect to its suitability to solving Scene Understanding problems.

Keywords: Description Logic, Deductive Reasoning, Scene Understanding, Scene Interpretation, Intersection Understanding, Road Recognition.

IV

Contents

List of Symbols   IX

1 Motivation   1
- 1.1 Intersection Understanding 2
  - 1.1.1 Definition 2
  - 1.1.2 Problem Characteristics 3
  - 1.1.3 Requirements 4
- 1.2 Knowledge-intensive AI 7
  - 1.2.1 Logic Programming 8
  - 1.2.2 Probabilistic Graphical Models 9
  - 1.2.3 Description Logic 11
- 1.3 Thesis Overview 12
  - 1.3.1 Outline 13
  - 1.3.2 Scope 14

2 Literature: Logic for Scene Understanding   17
- 2.1 Early Approaches 17
- 2.2 Group-by-Group Survey 18
  - 2.2.1 DCS, University of Toronto, Canada 18
  - 2.2.2 STS, Techn. University of Hamburg-Harburg, Germany . 19
  - 2.2.3 Matsuyama Lab, Kyoto, Japan 20
  - 2.2.4 School of Computing, University of Leeds, UK 21
  - 2.2.5 Department of Computing, Imperial College London, UK 22
  - 2.2.6 IAKS, University of Karlsuhe, Germany 22
  - 2.2.7 DIS, University of Rome, Italy 23
- 2.3 Related Approaches 23

| 2.4 | Discussion | 24 |

3 Description Logic (DL) — 27

3.1	DL-based Knowledge Representation Systems	27
3.2	DL Knowledge Bases	29
3.2.1	The TBox	29
3.2.2	The ABox	32
3.2.3	Semantics	34
3.3	DL Inference Services	36
3.3.1	TBox Inference	36
3.3.2	ABox Inference	37
3.4	Rules	40

4 DL Formalisation of Scene Understanding — 43

4.1	Formalisation of Data Input	43
4.1.1	Partial vs. Complete Data	44
4.1.2	Single vs. Distributed Sensor Setup	50
4.2	Modelling of Scene Geometry	54
4.2.1	Object Geometry	54
4.2.2	Relative Object Pose	56
4.2.3	Relational Scene Geometry	61
4.3	Formalisation of Scene Understanding Tasks	66
4.3.1	Object Detection: KB Realization	66
4.3.2	Object Classification: KB Realization	67
4.3.3	Link Prediction: Entailment	69
4.3.4	Data Association: Unification	70
4.4	Summary	70

5	**RONNY: The Road Network Ontology**		**73**
	5.1	Symbol Grounding	73
		5.1.1 Taxonomy of SceneObjects	74
		5.1.2 Taxonomy of GeometricPrimitives	76
		5.1.3 Taxonomy of spatialRelations	77
		5.1.4 Taxonomy of Functionality and functionalRelations	84
		5.1.5 Defined Concepts	85
	5.2	Intersection Geometry Model	87
		5.2.1 Object Geometry	87
		5.2.2 Scene Geometry	87
	5.3	Road Building Regulations	89
		5.3.1 Right-handed Traffic	90
		5.3.2 Dividers	91
		5.3.3 Driving Directions	92
		5.3.4 Bicycle/Car/Emergency Lanes	92
		5.3.5 Driveable Paths	94
		5.3.6 Geometry of Paths	95
6	**Application: DL-based Intersection Understanding**		**97**
	6.1	Sensor Setup	98
		6.1.1 Digital Map	99
		6.1.2 Positioning Sensor and Map Matching	102
		6.1.3 Stereo Camera	103
	6.2	Intersection Sample Set	105
	6.3	Experimental Results	112
		6.3.1 Example	114
		6.3.2 Model Validation	118
		6.3.3 Object Classification	119
		6.3.4 Object Detection	122
		6.3.5 Data Association	122
	6.4	Summary	123

7 Conclusion **125**

    7.1 Summary 125

    7.2 Evaluation: Description Logic for Scene Understanding 126

    7.3 Outlook 129

        7.3.1 Hypothesis Formation: Model Construction 129

        7.3.2 Probabilistic Logic Learning 131

Bibliography **133**

List of Symbols

Acronyms

AI	Artificial Intelligence
API	Application Programming Interface
ASP	Answer Set Programming
BBN	Bayesian Belief Network
CWA	Closed World Assumption
DIG	DL Implementation Group
DL	Description Logic
DL ABox	Part of a DLKB that contains assertional axioms only
DL TBox	Part of a DLKB that contains terminological axioms only
DLKB	Description Logic Knowledge Base
FOL	First Order Predicate Logic
GUI	Graphical User Interface
JEPD Semantics	Jointly Exhaustive and Pairwise Disjoint Semantics
HTTP	Hypertext Transfer Protocol
KR	Knowledge Representation
KB	Knowledge Base
LP	Logic Programming
MRF	Markov Random Field
OWA	Open World Assumption
OWL	Web Ontology Language
RONNY	Road Network Ontology
UNA	Unique Name Assumption
UTM Coordinates	Universal Transverse Mercator Coordinates
XML	Extensible Markup Language

For reference to the abbreviations for particular DL dialects, like e. g. $\mathcal{SHIQ}$, see Section 3.2.1.

Notational Conventions

Concepts	**Concept**, first letter is always capitalised
Roles	role, first letter is never capitalised
Individuals	*ind*, first letter is never capitalised
Template	$\mathcal{T}_{TEMPLATENAME}$

Concepts, roles and individuals, that are used as placeholders within a Template, are indicated by an underscore, as in **Concept**, role and *ind*.

Synonyms

The following terms are used interchangeably:

Image Understanding, Scene Understanding and Scene Interpretation
Intersection and Junction
Concept, Class and Type
Super- and Parent
Sub- and Child
Relation and Role
Instance and Individual

1 Motivation

"The time has come to reunify AI and Vision."
Takeo Kanade at the opening speech of the 2003 Conference on Computer Vision and Pattern Recognition.

The field of *Artificial Intelligence* (AI) was born at the famous 1956 Dartmouth Summer Research Conference which was organised and attended by a small group of renowned researchers – among them John McCarthy, Marvin Minsky, Claude Shannon, Allan Newell and Herbert Simon. The conference proposal included the goal to endow computers with information-processing capabilities comparable to those of biological systems (see (McCorduck 1979, p. 93)). As part of this, the field should develop "eyes and ears for the computer" (Selfridge 1955). The field of *Computer Vision* was born.

The early years of Computer Vision were dominated by *Image Understanding*, also called high-level vision. Initially, the problem was expected to be solved within a few months. To identify and solve its subtasks, the blocks world problem was set up: An image of an artificial scene consisting of a configuration of a stack of blocks should be interpreted by a program, so that the blocks' edges were labelled according to their correct physical configuration (Roberts 1965). However, promising microworld results turned out inapplicable in natural scenes. After more than a decade of research, not even low-level line extraction had been robustly solved ((Hanson and Riseman 1978) provide a representative overview). Abandoning the original Image Understanding goal, research for several years focussed on low-level vision. Computer Vision became independent from AI.

AI research, on the other hand, intensely focused on knowledge representation and reasoning formalisms. Over time, a transition occurred from so-called weak methods, which aim at general solutions to search problems with little or no domain assumptions, to strong methods, so-called knowledge-intensive systems (see e. g. (Russell and Norvig 1995)). A large number of representation and reasoning languages were developed, among them Semantic Nets (Quillian 1967), Planner (Hewitt 1969), Prolog (Colmerauer et al. 1972), and Frames (Minsky 1975). Probability theory resurged through the invention of the Bayesian Net formalism (Pearl 1988). Description Logics (Brachman and Levesque 1984) and Answer Set Programming (Gelfond and Lifschitz 1988) became established as contemporary successors of the early logic formalisms.

From the late seventies up to today, Computer Vision has gradually shifted its focus towards single object recognition in natural scenes, i. e. mostly a mid-level problem. Tremendous progress in terms of recognition rates and robustness to changing environment conditions has been made both on low- and mid-level problems, with a recent boost in the last half decade (see e. g. results obtained by (Leibe et al. 2008a)). In the above quote, Takeo Kanade argues that Computer Vision is now mature enough to reapproach the original AI goal of Image Understanding.

The present thesis aims for Image Understanding for the particular subclass of sensor images which depict road intersections, therefore termed *Intersection Understanding*. Two questions might now arise: 1. What exactly is Intersection Understanding? And 2. How can AI's focus on knowledge-intensive systems help in solving the Intersection Understanding problem?

1.1 Intersection Understanding

1.1.1 Definition

Generally speaking, Intersection Understanding is the subproblem of Image Understanding where the image to be interpreted depicts (a part of) a road intersection. However, varying definitions of the term Image Understanding exist. Any definition faces the difficulty that the amount of understanding reached by a system cannot be measured objectively by a human, who inherently interprets himself. Therefore, this thesis adopts an operational definition, which provides the benefit of testability. It is formulated in analogy to (Neumann 2003)'s definition of Image Understanding.

Definition 1.1 (Intersection Understanding)**.** Intersection Understanding is the reconstruction and interpretation of an arbitrary real-world scene of intersecting roads by means of sensor data, so that at least one of the following operational services can be accomplished:

- *(i)* Output of a natural language intersection description.
- *(ii)* Answering of conceptual queries about the intersection.
- *(iii)* Output of the set of topological path plans that is in accordance with legal road traffic rules.
- *(iv)* Output of the set of geometric path plans (trajectories) which keep lanes.

The present thesis makes contributions in the three latter services.

1.1. INTERSECTION UNDERSTANDING

1.1.2 Problem Characteristics

A particular subproblem of Intersection Understanding, namely road recognition, has been extensively studied. (Kastrinaki et al. 2003) and (McCall and Trivedi 2006) provide an overview. In contrast to Image Understanding, such systems solely deal with geometric reconstruction, thus aiming for Understanding task *(iv)* only.

The typical approach to road recognition is to first extract contour and/or region based cues (edges, their aggregation to lane markings, road texture, ...) from images from an onboard vision sensor. Based on these cues a generic road geometry model of low dimensionality[1] is instantiated. The search window for image cues at the next time step is constrained by this parameter estimate. An additionally available model of the vehicle dynamics can be used for smoothing the parameter estimates over time.

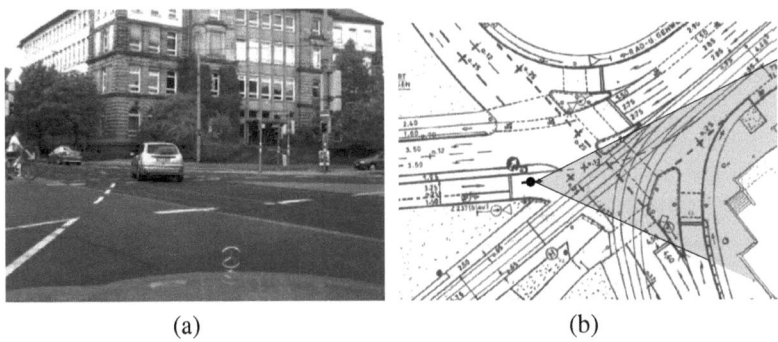

(a)   (b)

Figure 1.1: **Inner city intersection**   1.1(a) image taken by an onboard camera with 50° opening angle, 1.1(b) map from land surveying office.

This class of algorithms has been applied successively to highly constrained domains like highways, or in the rare cases that consider intersections, to some very particular and simple type of intersection (cf. (Hummel et al. 2007)). Their scalability to less constrained domains has not been demonstrated yet, even though first approaches date back to the early 1980s. Urban road intersection pose some particular challenges here (see Fig. 1.1):

- The abundance of existing intersection geometries necessitates a high-dimensional parameter space.

---

[1] A typical representation of a road is a *clothoid*. Its projection onto the image plane is typically approximated by a second or third order polynomial.

- A large part of the intersection does not enter the field of view of a standard onboard camera during traversal.

- Dense traffic and inner-city infrastructure lead to a massive amount of occlusion of relevant image clues.

- Frequently omitted markings on the intersection lead to a lack of image cues.

- The presence of an abundance of unmodelled objects feed as noise into the estimation process.

- Worse road quality, more variations in marking shape, and more rapidly changing environment conditions (lighting, ...) make cue detection more difficult.

One reason for the limited progress on less constrained domains is that a reduced and noisy amount of available image cues contrasts with the necessity of a high-dimensional parameter space. Applying the above class of algorithms therefore results in an *under-determined* estimation problem.

An alternative approach is required which can compute a unique solution within a high dimensional parameter space when only a sparse set of noisy features is available. Moreover, the parameter space itself for arbitrary intersections does not yet exist and must be developed.

1.1.3 Requirements

Deriving from these observations, the following paragraphs list a non-exhaustive set of prerequisites on a parameter space (termed *representation* below) and on a *reasoning formalism* for Intersection Understanding.

Reasoning Requirements

The reasoning formalism must provide means to drastically narrow down the set of solutions with respect to the Intersection Understanding tasks *(i)-(iv)* (Sec. 1.1.1), going beyond the obvious usage of the image cues. This can be achieved by imposing *constraints* and by computing *task-specific* solutions.

Constraints from Background Knowledge The term background knowledge includes common sense knowledge (as e. g. naive laws of physics) as well as task- or domain-specific knowledge (e. g. about a stopping line on a road). Its level

1.1. INTERSECTION UNDERSTANDING

of detail might range from quantitative low-level knowledge (like the typical appearance of that stopping line in terms of vision cues) to high-level conceptual knowledge (cars have to stop completely in front of stopping lines; after a stopping line there is usually a junction or/and a pedestrian crossing). Background knowledge is applied extensively and subconsciously by the human driver when traversing an intersection. This procedure might be crucial for yielding a feasibly small solution space.

Background knowledge can either be manually coded by a human knowledge engineer, or learned. Both approaches have their justification; a novice human driver will learn by gaining driving experience him/herself, as well as by listening to a teacher ("Your car must come to a complete stop in front of a stopping line!"). Although learning is more appealing from an algorithmic viewpoint because manual intervention is not required, a pure reinforcement-style learning algorithm would both require an excessive amount of training and exhibit bad driving behaviour during that training. However, only high-level qualitative concepts/rules are suitable for teaching by language. A reasoning formalism should therefore be able to incorporate manually coded high-level knowledge, as well as learn by itself.

Applying experience-based background knowledge to make up for lacking vision cues amounts to hypothesisation. This however implies that the arrival of new evidence will sometimes lead to the withdrawal of hypotheses. This process, known as *belief revision*, should be supported by a reasoner.

Constraints through Collective Computation Constraints can also be derived from a mutual, iterative exchange of partial results across algorithms which share common parameters. This principle has recently become known in the classification literature as *parameter tying* through *collective classification*, but the idea also extends to other Scene Understanding tasks. As an example, the tasks of lane recognition, localisation, and tracking of other cars are heavily intertwined; a joint solution is likely to be better than solving each task in isolation.

Task-driven Computation Task-driven computation refers to computing solutions only for those parameters of a parameter space that are relevant for solving a particular task or answering a particular query. For example, if the task at hand is "Turn right at the upcoming intersection!", then information about the types of lane markings will only be relevant concerning the current and the prospective ego-lane, but not concerning that intersection's left crossroad. A task-driven solution can drastically improve the parameter-feature-ratio.

Finally, to enable joint use of feature-, constraint- and task-based knowledge, which naturally come from very different abstraction levels, information must be excessively propagated along the abstraction hierarchy. In other words, a *combined bottom-up/top-down* reasoner is required.

Representational Requirements

The Intersection Understanding tasks *(i)* - *(iii)* require semantic knowledge and thus necessitate a transition from a purely geometric to a *semantics-enriched* parameter space. And, as outlined in the previous paragraph, task *(iv)* most likely requires semantic constraints as well. As the semantic knowledge is at least partially encoded by human knowledge engineers (see previous paragraph), a readable, maintainable and interchangeable representation is favourable. This in turn requires an *explicit, unambiguous* and *modular* representation: Intuitively, explicitness refers to explication of the relevant domain knowledge by a domain expert, as opposed to implicit coding by a programmer within, for example, a C++-function[2]. Ambiguity arises when two knowledge engineers assume different meanings behind a concept name, and the chance of ambiguities is minimised by a language with a formally well-defined semantics. Modularisation refers to a programming methodology in which semantically connected information is also grouped together syntactically[3].

Data from widely different abstraction layers must be incorporated (ranging from low-level vision cues to high-level rules like "give way!"), and the domain exhibits a rich relational structure (an appropriate explanation of the semantics of a stopping line involves the concepts lane, car and junction). Therefore, instead of the common so-called "flat" representations, a *hierarchical* and *relational* representation is preferred.

Furthermore, a representation of the instances of the parameter space must allow for *incomplete* data, that is, the value of some parameters might be unknown, because sensing is typically highly partial (see Section 1.1.2). The representation should also allow for *uncertain* input, as sensing is inherently noisy.

Finally, the parameter space must be *generic*, as the number and types of scene objects and their relations typically varies between intersections (an intersection consisting of four crossing roads has more degrees of freedom than one with two), and depending on the posed task or query.

Knowledge Engineering Requirements

Intersection Understanding in urban areas spans many domains, such as geometry, road markings, traffic signs, traffic rules for right of way, types and typical behaviour of traffic participants, tram lines, interest points like gas stations and

---

[2] A much further elaborated definition of the terms *explicitness* and *implicitness* of a representation is given by (Davies 2001).
[3] This is also called a *structured representation* in the literature.

restaurants, and so on. Incorporating such domain knowledge will at least partially be done by human domain experts (see second last paragraph).

A formal representation formalism must therefore come with an implementation which is capable of handling a large axiom set, and which allows the integration of several independently developed knowledge bases. As reasoning has turned out to be a computationally highly demanding task in any strictly formal language, the implementation must be based on a line of research on highly *optimised* reasoning.

Such a large-scale knowledge base project requires sound knowledge engineering techniques, just as large software projects have been found to crucially depend on good software engineering practices. This must be supported by the formalism itself –for example through an *object-oriented* paradigm, by the implementation infrastructure, and by knowledge engineering literature. The implementation infrastructure must provide *tools for code inspection*, such as graphical user interfaces (GUI) for visualisation and debuggers to find modelling errors. It should also include *"syntactic sugar"* for the language to enable concise and compact coding. Integration with other programming languages and/or databases should be supported by application programming interfaces (API). Knowledge engineering *literature* should be available to provide guidance on good code development practices.

Prototypical and beta implementations are not capable of satisfying the above requirements. Instead, language and implementations must have *matured* over years, being supported by an active user and developer community. Database technology, as an example, took about 10-15 years to progress from theoretical research in 1970 to the first robust implementations, and another 10 years to sophisticated end user tool support.

1.2 Knowledge-intensive AI

A *knowledge-intensive system* represents and manipulates a large *knowledge-base (KB)*. A KB is a body of explicit, high-level, and often also relational knowledge, represented in a symbolic notation readable by humans[4]. This closely matches the above identified requirements for an Intersection Understanding system. However, although a large set of formalisms for this system family has been developed by the AI community, no existing formalism has yet turned out to be the silver bullet for Scene Understanding.

---

[4]However, there does not seem to exist an agreed-upon definition of the term *knowledge-intensive system* in the literature.

There is also a considerable difference between theoretical research in a representational formalism, and research in knowledge engineering based on such a formalism. Past research has almost exclusively addressed the former, while strong computational limitations of language and implementations, lack of mature implementations and tool support prevented research on the latter (cf. the "Knowledge Engineering Requirements" in the last paragraph)[5]. By contrast, research in object-oriented software engineering, a task that can be considered comparably challenging, has produced a vast amount of written guidance for the users of the technique (as one prominent example cf. the book on software design patterns by (Gamma et al. 1995)). The last decade, however, has witnessed a gradual change of some of these determining factors.

Subsequently, closer examination will be given to a subset of formalisms, an available implementation of which has by now reached a provably stable, optimised and workable state. This must be demonstrated by an active user and developer community, and by a number of successful applications. They are grouped into the three families of Logic Programming, Description Logics, and graphical models.

1.2.1 Logic Programming

In very general terms, *Logic Programming (LP)* is the use of mathematical logic for computer programming. The LP semantics underlies a set of commercially relevant rule systems, among them Prolog, SQL relational databases, some production systems, and the proposals for rule languages for the Semantic Web (Grosof et al. 2003). LP is based on Horn clause logic, which is a restricted subset of First Order Logic (FOL). While full FOL is a very expressive formalism with a clearly defined semantics, for which sound and complete proof procedures exist, it is computationally intractable since proof termination is not guaranteed. Such a formalism is called undecidable[6]. LP constitutes a compromise between expressiveness and tractability by allowing only FOL formulas that are Horn clauses. A Horn clause is a rule like hasFather(x,y) ∧ hasBrother(y,z) → hasUncle(x,z), which has at most one predicate (in this case hasUncle) in the rule consequence.

Pure LP provides the benefits of adhering to the well-defined semantics of FOL, and of being fully declarative. The declarative paradigm, as opposed to the procedural one that is inherent to widespread programming languages like C++ or Java, expresses exclusively "what" should be achieved, whereas the "how", i. e. the

---

[5]This is true for knowledge engineering for the purpose of enabling automated reasoning. It is not true for knowledge engineering for data storage purposes, which is both a much simpler task and addressed in many works

[6]The terms *soundness*, *completeness*, and *decidability* will be formally introduced in Chapter 3.

control flow, is completely intrinsic to the reasoner. Although there is an ongoing philosophical controversy between the representatives of the two paradigms (its beginnings are traced in (Winograd 1985)), it is widely accepted that a mostly declarative formalism provides for the above identified requirements of explicitness, non-ambiguity and modularity of a KB. However, pure LP still exhibits poor computational performance on realistic KBs[7].

For improving performance, the *Prolog* interpreter sacrifices full declarativity for user-defined procedural search heuristics. A reordering of clauses in Prolog can therefore cause drastic changes in program behaviour. This hampers maintenance (e. g. insertion of a new formula) and modularised KB development. The formalism nevertheless remains undecidable, and a non-terminating program can be written in just one line of code. The biggest shortcoming of Prolog with respect to Scene Understanding is its closed world semantics: It assumes by default that the available information is complete, assigning truth value "false" to all non-specified information. This contrasts with the inherent incompleteness of knowledge acquired by a sensor (see Section 1.1.2).

More recently, *Answer Set Programming (ASP)* emerged as a purely declarative alternative to Prolog. Whereas in Prolog, the solutions to a query are yielded by proving valid substitutions of the query variables using the KB, the ASP paradigm defines the KB's stable logical models (called answer sets) as the solution set (Gelfond and Lifschitz 1988). ASP allows both open and closed world predicates, making it suitable to represent incomplete as well as complete information. Its roots are in work on non-monotonic reasoning, the lack of which has long been identified as a shortcoming of FOL (cf. the special issue vol. 13 of the AI Journal 1980). A monotonic formalism cannot invalidate any previously drawn conclusion, i. e. it disallows belief revision. ASP is as well decidable. The last 10 years witnessed a quick growth in the ASP user community. Developers begin to claim that the leading solvers DLV[8] and SMODELS[9] are efficient and mature enough for dealing with large datasets. (Baral 2003) provides a proof of concept for modularised ASP programming by introducing a couple of programming templates.

1.2.2 Probabilistic Graphical Models

Probabilistic graphical models offer a consistent treatment of uncertainty through the use of probability theory. The two most common types of graphical models

---

[7] The LP community uses the term *logic program* instead of KB. The term KB will nevertheless be used throughout this text for maintaining consistency.
[8] DLV: www.dbai.tuwien.ac.at/proj/dlv/
[9] SMODELS: www.tcs.hut.fi/Software/smodels/

are *Bayesian Belief Networks (BBN)* and *Markov Networks*, also called *Markov Random Fields (MRF)*.

Representationally, a BBN/MRF is a directed/undirected graph, each node of which corresponds to a random variable $Y_i, i \in 1,..,n$, and the set of (lacking) edges encodes a set of conditional independence assumptions between these variables. Through exploitation of the local independencies, such a graph compactly represents a family of joint probability distributions over the set of random variables $\mathbf{Y} = Y_1, \ldots, Y_n$. Together with an additional parameter set –conditional probability distributions for each node in the case of the BBN, and a set of potential functions for the MRF– it uniquely determines a joint distribution $P(\mathbf{Y})$.

One common inference task for graphical models is to compute the posterior probability distribution over a set of query variables $\mathbf{X} \subset \mathbf{Y}$, given the information $\mathbf{e}$ about a set of evidence variables $\mathbf{E} \subset \mathbf{Y}$, that is $P(\mathbf{X}|\mathbf{E}=\mathbf{e})$. Another common task is to find the maximum posterior estimate (MAP) for the values of $\mathbf{X}$ given the evidence: $\text{argmax}_{\mathbf{x}} P(\mathbf{X} = \mathbf{x} | \mathbf{E} = \mathbf{e})$. For graphs with low treewidth, efficient exact inference procedures can be applied. Otherwise exact inference is intractable, but efficient approximate methods, such as Markov Chain Monte Carlo sampling, have been developed. The reasoning allows for belief revision in the presence of additional evidence, also known as "explaining away evidence" here. Furthermore, the graphical model framework allows for learning of both parameters and network structure, also known as model selection.

Graphical models thus offer a strong reasoning framework and oftentimes efficient algorithms, but they severely suffer from the representational limitation that they can only represent propositional statements. A propositional language, as opposed to a first-order one, does not commit to the existence of objects and relations (cf. here also e.g. Sec. 14.6 in (Russell and Norvig 1995)). By consequence, generalising statements about the domain ("A man with a child is a father.") cannot be separated from knowledge about individuals ("Emily is John's child."), and relations between individuals cannot be properly expressed. This results in vastly more cumbersome domain descriptions and limits reasoning strength. Furthermore, network topology must be redesigned by hand whenever the problem instance changes (e. g. an intersection with two crossroads may have many more unknowns than one with one crossroad).

These limitations are addressed by recent research forming under the name of *Probabilistic Logic Learning / Statistical Relational Learning*, which aims at using FOL as a template for automatically constructing a graphical model in which reasoning then takes place. A formula written in FOL maps to a family of graphical model topologies. The exact model topology is determined by the particular constants (like "Emily") the formula is instantiated with. Reasoning is then performed within the probabilistic framework. Thereby the representational strength of FOL is combined with the inferential strength offered by probabilistic graphical models. Although a promising approach, the available implementations were not mature enough at the time of writing to be applied here.

1.2.3 Description Logic

Research in *Description Logic (DL)* emerged in the 1980s –then under the label *Terminological Systems*– as a consequence of the experienced shortcomings of Semantic Nets and Frames (Brachman and Levesque 1984). Those had been designed for intuitive, ad hoc specification of knowledge and reasoning procedures, but lacked a precise underlying semantics. Seemingly identical components therefore exhibited differing behaviour, leading to difficulties in KB maintenance and integration (Baader et al. 2003). DL aims at minimising ambiguities by adhering to FOL semantics, while retaining as much intuitivity as possible. Modern DL dialects are proven decidable yet expressive subsets of $\mathcal{L}^2$, the FOL over at most two variables that allows for unary and binary predicates (e. g. Father(x) and hasChild(x,y), respectively). For readability, DL adopts a variable-free notation, e. g. Father $\equiv$ Man $\sqcap$ $\exists$hasChild ("A father is a man that has a child."), and it supports an object-oriented approach to KB engineering (see the (W3C Working Group Note 2006)). DL makes an open world assumption, therefore allowing for incomplete knowledge. It also makes an open domain assumption, which allows the set of specified individuals to be incomplete. Pure DL is also fully declarative.

The Semantic Web initiative boosted development and use of DL implementations and knowledge engineering tools. In 2004, DL became the underlying formalism of the OWL DL Web Ontology Language, which is a W3C (World Wide Web Consortium) recommendation and thus a de facto web standard (W3C Recommendation 2004). A set of optimised and continuously maturing reasoners for expressive and decidable DL dialects are now available, among them FACT++, KAON2, PELLET and RACERPRO. The same holds for development and visualisation tools, two examples of which are the OWL tool PROTÉGÉ and RACERPORTER, the GUI to RACERPRO[10]. As an indication of the size of the user community, the search engine for OWL ontologies SWOOGLE[11] to date lists more than 10.000 entries. Furthermore, the Semantic Web fostered research on integration of KBs from heterogenous sources (e.g. (Borgida and Serafini 2003)), which is why KB integration is by now most likely understood better under OWL DL than under any other formal representation.

---

[10]For corresponding references, see Chapter 3.
[11]SWOOGLE: http://swoogle.umbc.edu//

On the downside, classic DL inference supports deductive and thus monotonic reasoning only (cf. Sec. 1.2.1). Research on non-monotonic language extensions is a main subject of present research. One line of research integrates DL with non-monotonic ASP (Schindlauer 2006), while another proposes abductive DL reasoning (see (Möller and Neumann 2008)). Both approaches offer prototypical implementations. A second limitation, which it shares with all logic-based formalisms, is its lacking expressiveness with regard to uncertain knowledge. It provides such functionality only rudimentarily through the $\exists$- and $\sqcup$ -constructors, but not through soft axioms.

Conclusion

According to the brief review above, three formalisms prequalified as feasible representation and reasoning formalisms for knowledge-intensive Scene Understanding. These are namely Answer Set Programming, Probabilistic Logic Learning, and Description Logic. Although appealing, Probabilistic Logic Learning was ruled out because the beta status of its implementations would hamper proper knowledge engineering. Both other formalisms are feasible. While Answer Set Programming offers non-monotonic reasoning, Description Logic seems the slightly more mature technology, with better tool support, and a larger developer and user community. Description Logic has been chosen as the reference language for the present thesis.

1.3 Thesis Overview

The present thesis investigates the feasibility of the Description Logic fragment of formal logic as a representation and reasoning technique for Scene Understanding.

There are a lot of yet unanswered questions with respect to logic-based Scene Understanding, including, but certainly not limited to the following: Is formal logic a suitable formalism for Scene Understanding at all? Which are the required properties of such a formalism? Which classical vision tasks (like object detection, object classification, data association, tracking, sensor data fusion, ...) map to which reasoning services (satisfiability, consistency, instance checking, retrieval, non-monotonic reasoning, ...)? Which kind of knowledge should be reasonably encoded and in what level of detail (e. g. qualitative, quantitative, or mixed knowledge)? What can the interface to the quantitative, geometric layer look like? How can geometry be represented at all? What logical paradigms do different types of sensory input (e.g. redundant vs. complementary, object vs. feature input) map to?

1.3. THESIS OVERVIEW 13

Can a combined bottom-up/top-down (with respect to abstraction layer) algorithm be designed?

The present thesis proposes answers to these questions. Some answers are given in a principled way and comprise so-called design patterns written in DL. Design patterns are intended for reuse and extension by users. Other answers are given empirically after performing and evaluating a detailed case study: A KB is developed in DL for the application domain of roads and their intersections. In a set of reasoning experiments, classic Computer Vision tasks are solved by classic DL reasoning, and the system's performance on these tasks is evaluated. The evaluation is performed on a set of complex, natural scenes using realistic sensor data.

To promote further research, the KB developed for this thesis, and all example intersection data, have been made available on `www.mrt.uni-karlsruhe.de/ronny`. The RACERPRO reasoner, which is free for academic usage, has been used for development and testing. Experimenting with new intersections and/or new sensors, as well as comments on modifications or extensions of the proposed design patterns, are highly welcome.

This project is situated within the larger research initiative SFB/TR 28 "Cognitive Automobiles" supported by the German research foundation DFG, the eventual goal of which is to enable driverless road driving.

1.3.1 Outline

Chapter 2 provides an up-to-date overview of existing literature on logic-based Scene Understanding. As it turns out, few groups work on the subject, and some of these use FOL only for representational purpose but not for reasoning, or operate in a microworld. A proof-by-implementation of the usefulness of logic for realistic Scene Understanding is therefore yet pending.

Chapter 3 gives an introduction into Description Logic with a focus on the particular dialect $\mathcal{SHIQ}$ which will be used throughout the remaining chapters. This chapter is basically a selective synthesis of Part I of (Baader et al. 2003) and a few other DL texts, enriched by examples from the Intersection Understanding domain.

Chapter 4 elaborates on principled ways of mapping several important Scene Understanding issues into a DL setting. At first, several types of sensor input data are mapped to a DL representation. These types are namely partial vs. complete input data, and single vs. distributed input data. Afterwards, a principled way of specifying qualitative scene geometry models in DL is proposed. Finally, several classic Scene Understanding tasks are mapped to suitable DL inference services. In particular, these are object detection and classification, link prediction and data association.

Chapter 5 introduces the **Ro**ad **N**etwork **O**ntology (RONNY). It is a DL TBox implemented in the dialect $\mathcal{SHIQ}$, which models the qualitative geometry and building regulations of road intersections for the purpose of Scene Understanding, making extensive use of the findings from Chapter 4.

Chapter 6 describes the automatic generation of a RONNY ABox out of sensor data from a digital map, a global positioning device and vision-based object detectors. Afterwards, DL reasoning is applied to several Scene Understanding tasks. These tasks are namely: In which directions is driving allowed on each lane (classification task)? Which traffic participants (bicycles, cars) are allowed on each lane (classification task)? Between which lane pairs does a driveable path exist (detection task)? Which of the map's lanes is equivalent to the lane the vehicle is driving on (data association task)? The performance of task solving was evaluated using a sample set of 23 complex, natural scene intersections from both urban areas and freeways in Germany.

Chapter 7 concludes with a qualitative evaluation of the overall suitability of the DL formalism for Scene Understanding.

1.3.2 Scope

The following issues are *not* covered in this contribution:

Computer Vision Although tremendously desirable, the development of Computer Vision algorithms for detection and classification of relevant intersection infrastructure would have exceeded the scope of this thesis.

Uncertainty As this thesis' focus is on knowledge engineering, a DL language with an existing implementation was chosen. Unfortunately, this ruled out the possibility of considering uncertainty. Undoubtedly, treatment of uncertainty is a prerequisite to any Scene Understanding system. The DL community is actively working towards a synthesis of probability theory and description logics, as e. g. the Dagstuhl workshop "Logic and Probability for Scene Interpretation" shows[12], which was co-organised by R. Möller, developer of the RACERPRO DL reasoner. Implementation efforts are under way (see e. g. (Möller and Näth 2008)).

Learning It is the author's personal opinion that learning will play an essential role in real world Scene Understanding tasks. However, to pave the way for a

---
[12] http://www.dagstuhl.de/08091

learning framework, suitable knowledge representation and reasoning formalisms need to be developed *first*. The formal logic formalism provides an excellent basis for learning, exemplified by the immense body of work on inductive Logic Programming (started by (Muggleton 1991)). Learning has also been addressed in a DL framework (e. g. (Cohen and Hirsh 1994)). However, an implementation of a mature learning DL reasoner is not available at present.

2 Literature: Logic for Scene Understanding

The following survey covers, to the best of the author's knowledge, publications up to spring 2008 in the field of logic-based Scene Understanding. In particular, approaches with the following characteristics are surveyed:

1. The knowledge representation language is formal logic.
2. The primary form of reasoning is formal logic inference.
3. The application focus is on perception (as opposed to, e. g., planning).

Taking into account the characteristics of a perception system for natural scenes from Chapter 1, a fourth characteristic can be derived from the third one above: The reasoning architecture should support bottom-up as well as top-down reasoning.

These characteristics rule out a large body of well-known early work on knowledge-based Image Understanding, which will briefly be mentioned in the next section.

2.1 Early Approaches

Expert systems, also termed *rule-based systems*, were the dominant representation scheme for a wide range of industrial applications in the 1980s. Expert systems typically represented knowledge in the form of *production rules*. These are simple rules of the form "IF *condition* THEN *action*", which have Horn clauses as a special case. In contrast to FOL, a special interpreter, which does not guarantee consistency or correctness[1], and is not transparent to the user, controls inferences on the rule-base. (Ballard and Brown 1982, p. 407), in line with many other researchers, argue that, in the end, expert systems have not met the expectations of an understandable, modular, and thus maintainable knowledge representation.

---
[1] This chapter makes use of some termini from DL and from FOL without explanation. See Chapter 3 and (Russell and Norvig 1995), respectively, for reference.

Today their use is limited to few niche applications. (Matsuyama 1989) gives an overview of work on expert-system-based image processing until the late 1980s.

Two other families of formerly popular image processing representations are Quillian's *Semantic Nets* and Minsky's *Frames* ((Quillian 1967) and (Minsky 1975)). Both had been designed to mimic human representation and reasoning, to provide for intuitive, ad hoc specification of knowledge and reasoning procedures. (Rao and Jain 1988) give an overview of systems based on these representations. In the end, however, those systems also turned out difficult to understand, maintain and integrate (e. g. (Baader et al. 2003, p. 2f)). By now they have been widely abandoned and replaced by languages with a precisely defined semantics in terms of subsets of FOL such as Description Logics.

2.2 Group-by-Group Survey

2.2.1 Department of Computer Science, University of Toronto, Canada

(Reiter and Mackworth 1989) provided the first definition of the problem of image interpretation in a logical framework. For the application of sketch map understanding, they showed how scene domain knowledge about geographic objects, extracted image domain cues in terms of lines and regions, and the depiction mapping between image and scene domain, can be represented using FOL. Their goal was a strictly bottom-up classification of the segmented image cues into the classes road, river, shore, land and water. They defined such an interpretation as a *logical model* of a set of FOL formulae.

In FOL, model computation is undecidable, and the number of models can be infinite. Reiter and Mackworth therefore made the grossly simplifying assumption of complete and noise-free image domain data, i. e. a complete, unambiguous and correct low-level segmentation of the image into meaningful lines and regions is assumed. Transferred to FOL, this amounts to assuming a *closed domain*, a *closed world* with respect to the image, and *unique names*. These assumptions allowed for converting the FOL formulae to propositional logic formulae. The set of logical models of these formulae was then computed by translation into a logically equivalent *constraint satisfaction problem*, for which efficient and well-understood solvers exist. The proposed approach was not implemented in a vision system.

2.2.2 Institute for Software Systems, Techn. University of Hamburg-Harburg, Germany

(Schröder 1999) and (Neumann and Möller 2006) advocate the use of Description Logic for Scene Interpretation. They state that neither *deductive* nor *abductive* reasoning alone are sufficient for reasoning about interpretations, and adopt Reiter's idea of *constructing* a *logical model*. However, they are content with *partial models* in that not all aspects of the scene must be expressed as formulae. While Schröder requires *maximally specific* modelling, Neumann and Möller advocate a level of detail that is *task-dependent*, as not all information seems relevant under all contexts.

Concerning image evidence, Schröder requires an initial segmentation which fully covers the image, while all further evidence may be incomplete. He follows Reiter's idea of noise-free data, as he requires the partial model to be consistent with all future evidence. Neumann and Möller in contrast argue that evidence is inherently partial which necessitates extensive hypothesisation. It must therefore be possible for later evidence to trigger the withdrawal of previous conclusions (although they leave open how this can be achieved). They thus implicitly advocate *non-monotonic* reasoning for Scene Interpretation.

Examining the required language expressiveness, Neumann and Möller conclude that at least the DL $\mathcal{ALCF(D)}$, which includes feature chain agreement and concrete domains, is necessary for Scene Interpretation. (Möller 2001) has, however, shown that the former constructor jeopardises decidability of reasoning for expressive DLs. Therefore (Möller and Neumann 2008) have recently described how decidability-preserving *rules* can function as an alternative to feature chains. Schröder, in contrast, advocates the use of a much more expressive DL (his proposal could be called an extension of $\mathcal{ALCQFRO(D)}$), thereby sacrificing *finite models* and *decidability*, and argues for the development of *approximate reasoning* methods instead to ensure termination.

For constructing the logical model, Schröder describes an extended variant of a Tableau Calculus, which is a procedure used in DL for proving satisfiability of concepts by model construction. Möller and Neumann are inspired by *Configuration technology* (cf. Section 2.3 on related approaches). Configuration systems support tasks where technical components have to be configured to form a system which meets given specifications. A typical configuration task is to configure a computer according to customer wishes. Close analogies between Configuration languages and DL languages had already been noticed by (Möller et al. 1996), and (Hotz and Neumann 2005) have elaborated on the similarities between Configuration and Scene Interpretation. Here, the focus is on mapping Configuration's algorithm building blocks to readily available DL inference services. They first conclude that already standard *deductive* DL reasoning is in principle capable of performing some of the required steps such as *classification* and *unification* (which they call instance specialisation and instance merging). Second, model construction cannot be realised solely based on classic DL inference, as it requires the creation of new individuals, backtracking from previously drawn conclusions, and preference measures during the search for interpretations. Therefore, they advocate building a *procedural framework* around the reasoning engine. For the special case of part-whole reasoning they show that the query language nRQL (Haarslev and Möller 2003) can be helpful in building such a framework.

In their most recent work, which is part of the BOEMIE project[2], (Möller and Neumann 2008) abandon model construction and turn towards a combination of *abductive* and *deductive* reasoning (see next paragraph for details) for interpretation of multimedia data. It can be seen as the first formal account of abductive-deductive DL ABox reasoning and as a successor of the work of (Poole 1989) on abductive-deductive reasoning in FOL. Images, text and video documents are used as input data. Some initial thoughts about *unification* of individuals are laid down as well. They have, however, not yet elaborated on an algorithmic architecture for Scene Interpretation on the basis of this reasoning framework.

2.2.3 Matsuyama Lab, Kyoto, Japan

(Matsuyama and Hwang 1985) aim for aerial Image Understanding. They define an image interpretation as the result of an incremental hypothesise-and-test procedure. A complete initial segmentation is not required a priori, but is incrementally constructed in the course of reasoning. *Classification* of detected image patches as well as *unification* reasoning is performed, i. e. two image patches can be merged into one domain object, both of which involve spatial reasoning and object appearance constraints.

The authors give a logical formulation of the reasoning procedure in the spirit of the abductive-deductive reasoning developed by (Poole 1989): Observations in the form of formalised sensor data are to be *explained* by the given domain knowledge and another set of formulae, the *hypothesis* or *theory* (abduction step). After adding the hypothesis to the set of formulae, the observations follow as a logical consequence (deduction step). Horn clauses are proposed as the underlying logical language.

However, it turns out that neither the logic language nor the reasoning procedure

---
[2]http://www.boemie.org/

are used in the implementation. A combination of frames and production rules is used in their place.

2.2.4 School of Computing, University of Leeds, UK

This group has a long history in combining continuous Computer Vision methods and formal logic representation and reasoning. An overview of recent projects can be found in (Cohn et al. 2006).

One focus is on learning qualitative spatiotemporal models of events in traffic scenes from video input. Initially, the field of view of a static camera is partitioned into regions based on extracted object trajectories. Event models describing the relative behaviour of moving objects are then built out of single frame descriptions of qualitative object relationships. Relative direction and direction of motion are used as spatial calculi. In later work this spatial vocabulary is not provided a priori, but learned in a data driven fashion. The resulting event model database has been used in the traffic domain to learn and recognise various event models, like following and overtaking, and to identify unusual behaviour. However, besides the rudimentary use of situation calculi predicates, formal logic has neither been used for representation nor for reasoning in this work.

Another ongoing project is autonomous learning of both low level (continuous) and high level (symbolic) models of objects and activity (Magee et al. 2004). The learned models drive an embodied (i.e. one which interacts with its environment) cognitive agent. The symbolic representation is explicitly grounded to the sensor data, and is learned through *Inductive Logic Programming* using Progol. First results demonstrate a game playing agent.

In a third project, (Bennett et al. 2008) demonstrate that a state-of-the-art statistical blob tracker and classifier shows significantly increased accuracy when enhanced by a subsequent logical analysis. A reasoner computes the set of logical models whose objects satisfy two simple spatio-temporal continuity formulae: (a) an object cannot be in more than one place at a time; (b) object movement must be continuous. This in particular allows for better disambiguation in the presence of object crowds. The reasoner is provided with the complete set of relevant scene objects (*closed domain assumption*). The best model is chosen according to a quantitative voting function. The reasoning is implemented in SICStus Prolog. The approach can be considered one of the rare cases where a logic-enhanced approach has been proven superior in terms of recognition rate. However, no comparison has been made by the authors with a state-of-the-art quantitative tracker, i. e. one that uses data association techniques to impose the same kind of spatiotemporal constraints such as (Leibe et al. 2008b).

2.2.5 Department of Computing, Imperial College London, UK

(Shanahan 2005) summarises the group's body of work on logic-based perception using abduction and deduction in combination. Their most recent work is implemented on LUDWIG, a basic upper-torso humanoid. Shanahan argues that perception, cognition, and action must act in concert to carry out what philosophers of science call *hypothetico-deductive reasoning*. First, the most promising hypotheses are formed that might explain the sensor data using abduction. Second, the consequences of these hypotheses are computed using deduction. Third, those expectations are tested through actions, i. e. by carrying out experiments. The value of a hypothesis is reduced if its expectations are unfulfilled, and vice versa. Consequently, Shanahan stresses the necessity of an *embodied* system, which not only passively manipulates symbols, but interacts with the environment and therefore gives meaning to the internal representation. Parts of the system have been implemented as an abductive meta-interpreter written in Prolog, which interfaces with low-level vision routines. It uses the event calculus as the underlying ontology. LUDWIG's vision routines currently seem restricted to edge detection. His reasoner finds the best explanation for a set of extracted lines, e. g. an image of a cube viewed from a certain perspective. Future work involves incorporation of a larger set of features like colour or stereo information.

2.2.6 Institut für Algorithmen und Kognitive Systeme, University of Karlsuhe, Germany

The group has introduced a conceptual representation for behavioural knowledge in the form of so-called Situation Graph Trees (SGT) (Arens and Nagel 2002). An SGT is a set of hierarchically ordered situation graphs. They in turn consist of situations and temporal transition edges between them. A situation is defined by a set of states which have to be fulfilled by an agent, and a set of possible actions. States regard the agent's dynamics (e.g. accelerating), its relation to other agents (e.g. overtaking) and its relation to infrastructure (e.g. approaching). States and actions are qualitative abstractions from quantitative vision data. The SGT is formalised using a fuzzy metric temporal Horn logic. A graph search algorithm finds the situation an agent is currently instantiating.

Although the representation is primarily used for bottom-up reasoning about agent behaviour, (Arens and Nagel 2005) demonstrated exemplarily how inferred qualitative behavioural knowledge can be used in a top-down manner to improve quantitative vehicle tracking on inner-city intersections. Tracking results, produced by a Kalman Filter from images of a stationary camera, are fed into the SGT to predict the next action. The resulting action predicates are refined down to a quantitative level and used to update the Kalman Filter's motion model. The authors qualitatively show that this is especially useful in the case of lacking image features, for example during partial or total vehicle occlusion. A quantitative comparison between tracking results from Kalman Filter-only and logic-enhanced processing has not been made.

2.2.7 Department of Computer and Systems Science, University of Rome, Italy

(Pirri and Finzi 1999) address *active perception* in a mobile robot manipulator setting. They sketch ideas for a unified formalisation of perception, inference, and actions within the *situation calculus*, which can be seen as an ontology for reasoning about actions and their effects in First Order Logic.

In their formulation, they introduce sensing actions as queries to an environmental sensor such as a camera, which yield so-called perceptibles. Using background knowledge and past perceptibles, they are combined to form more complex perceptibles. These are in turn used to choose the next sensing action, which aims at maximising information gain.

The approach has been implemented on three mobile manipulators using Golog and Prolog (Finzi et al. 2001). The focus of this work however is on the action side rather than on the Computer Vision side.

2.3 Related Approaches

Some related approaches might also prove valuable in the context of logic-based Scene Interpretation.

The *KOGS Lab* at Hamburg University focusses on Scene Interpretation based on Configuration technology (e. g. (Terzić et al. 2007)). They incrementally reconstruct a scene by building hypotheses based on vision features and background knowledge about the scene, which is formulated within an ontology. The approach is relevant to logic-based Scene Interpretation for several reasons: First, in contrast to many logic-based approaches, a working prototype SCENIC has been demonstrated to enhance state-of-the-art Computer Vision algorithms. Second, Configuration languages are close to Description Logics. Third, SCENIC has a model construction algorithm on offer which could possibly be modified towards logical model construction.

The *ORION group* at Inria Sophia-Antipolis pursues an approach to spatio-temporal scenario representation and recognition for video surveillance (Bremond et al. 2006), which has been extensively tested. Although the developed representation and reasoning framework is not based on logic, it is of interest in terms of ontology design.

The *NIST* (National Institute of Standards and Technology) has pursued some preliminary work on using Description Logic to reason about potential damages incurred by collisions between an autonomous vehicle and other objects (Provine et al. 2004).

Some other, related fields display a more vivid interest in formal logic: In *image retrieval*, the development of languages for representing and querying image content is currently subject of intensive research. (Saathoff and Staab 2008), for example, demonstrate how a conceptual description of image regions and typical spatial relations can help in retrieving and labelling image regions. This community is in the process of developing large image retrieval knowledge bases, which should be examined with respect to their applicability in the Scene Interpretation context. Logic-based approaches developed within the *RoboCup* community inevitably have to address the intricate issues of real-time performance and input data uncertainty, which are relevant in the Computer Vision context. As an example, (Lattner 2007) from TZI, Bremen University, has developed a rule learning approach based on Prolog for discovering and predicting player behaviour patterns. Finally, some work on qualitative reasoning has been pursued in the field of dynamic *robot localisation*, e. g. by (Wagner et al. 2004).

2.4 Discussion

A considerable number of Computer Vision researchers have recommended the use of qualitative knowledge representations for high-level Scene Interpretation, among them (McCarthy and Hayes 1969) in the early days, later (Rao and Jain 1988), and, more recently, (Shah 2004) and (Kanade 2006). Early representations, like expert systems, semantic nets and frames, were unconvincing due to lack of formality. Rigorously formal representations, on the other hand, have so far only rarely been applied (fewer than 10 groups worldwide to the best of the author's knowledge). Reiter's pioneering logical formalisation of a vision problem, and later Schröder's DL-based formalisation, made unrealistic assumptions concerning the vision routines and therefore were not adopted by the Computer Vision community. Later FOL-based approaches, like Pirri's, focused more on the action side than on the sensing side of perception, and solved planning problems using

2.4. DISCUSSION 25

the situation calculus or the event calculus as the underlying ontology. From the set of presented approaches, only (Arens and Nagel 2005), (Magee et al. 2004), (Bennett et al. 2008), (Shanahan 2005), (Neumann and Möller 2006) and (Möller and Neumann 2008) turned out to classify as logic-based Computer Vision according to the criteria defined above.

Logical Principles Applied

While Reiter uses a full first order representation, most other approaches use the Horn-clause subset as used by Prolog. Magee is the only representative using inductive Logic Programming. Recently, with the development of expressive and at the same time tractable languages, Description Logic has become fashionable.

Most approaches impose a closed domain assumption, i. e. they introduce all possible scene objects a priori. Approaches which consider sensor uncertainty or multiple sensors realised the need to abandon the unique name assumption. All systems seem to implicitly or explicitly assume finite logical models of the scene. With the exception of Reiter's early work, all systems seem to assume an open world, i. e. pay attention to the fact that visual evidence in general is incomplete.

All approaches view the resulting Scene Interpretation as a logical model of the knowledge base, but they vary in the way this model is constructed: No system solely relies on deduction. While some use abduction to hypothesise new formulae, others hand the construction problem over to a non-logic formalism like constraint satisfaction or build a procedural framework around a deductive reasoner. When a full scene reconstruction is envisaged, abduction cannot be used in isolation, but must be combined with deduction and/or a procedural framework.

The Status Quo

Logic-enhanced systems have not yet proven their superiority over state-of-the-art quantitative Computer Vision in terms of recognition or classification rates (although Bennett and Arens come close). It has furthermore not yet been convincingly demonstrated that the use of logic enhances the transparency of incorporated knowledge or of drawn conclusions (due to explicitness, modularity and semantic unambiguity). These advantages can – if present – only become quantifiable with the development of large logic-based Computer Vision knowledge bases (otherwise simple if-then rules in the source code do, indeed, suffice).

3 Description Logic

Description Logic (DL) is a synonym for a family of object-oriented knowledge representation (KR) formalisms that separate background knowledge about an application domain (intensional knowledge) from knowledge about particular individuals within that domain (extensional knowledge). Databases, in contrast, solely capture extensional knowledge. A full First Order Logic knowledge base, on the other hand, does not make this particular distinction and is not object-oriented. The terms *terminological systems, concept languages* and *term-subsumption systems* are older synonyms for DL. As the name indicates, DL is equipped with a formal, declarative semantics, making it equivalent to a set of FOL axioms.

The axiomatisation of intensional knowledge in a DL, together with its precise semantics, allows for *deductive reasoning*: Knowledge, which is contained implicitly in a DL knowledge base (DLKB), is made explicit through inferences. Reasoning algorithms used in modern DL systems have been proven to be *sound* and *complete*, i.e. any result is guaranteed to be correct and exhaustive. In contrast to FOL theorem provers or systems based on Horn clauses with function symbols, such as Prolog, DL reasoning is *decidable*. This means that there exists a reasoning algorithm that terminates with an answer after a finite number of steps.

After an introduction into the architecture of DL-based KR systems in Section 3.1, the syntax and semantics of a wide class of DL languages will be provided in Section 3.2, accompanied by a set of examples from the application domain of road network modelling. Section 3.3 describes classical DL reasoning services. Much recent research effort is currently spent on enhancing these deductive reasoning capabilities. Two pragmatic enhancements which are available in current reasoning technology, trigger rules and other so-called procedural extensions, are briefly mentioned in Section 3.4.

This chapter is intended to serve as reference for syntax and semantic of the DL expressions used in subsequent chapters.

3.1 DL-based Knowledge Representation Systems

A DL-based *knowledge representation system* is an implementation of a reasoning system for DL knowledge bases. It connects to a knowledge-intensive application or to an end user via an interface to set up the knowledge base, to manipulate it, and to reason about its content. The interface can come in the form of an application programming interface (API) or a graphical user interface (GUI). Figure 3.1 sketches a typical software architecture.

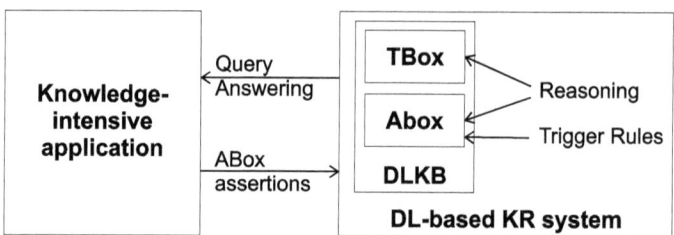

Figure 3.1: Architecture of a knowledge-intensive application based on Description Logic. The application states new facts in the form of ABox assertions (see next Section), which are added to the DLKB. The KR system uses the DLKB to answer queries through deductive reasoning, that are posed by the application.

Among the leading modern KR systems are FACT++ [1], KAON2[2], PELLET[3] and RACERPRO[4]. The application described in this contribution is based on RACERPRO 1.9.3.

All mentioned KR systems provide a DIG-compliant API (DIG is short for DL Implementation Group). The DIG standard comprises an XML-specification for DL languages, ask/tell functionality, along with a HTTP-based communication protocol, and support for multiple knowledge bases. It enables distributed, client/server architectures for knowledge-intensive applications.

A widely used GUI is the open source tool PROTÉGÉ[5], which connects to a reasoner via DIG. It uses OWL (Web Ontology Language) as the underlying language, which corresponds to the DL language $\mathcal{SROIQ}(\mathcal{D})$ in the case of OWL 1.1, and to $\mathcal{SHOIN}(\mathcal{D})$ in the case of OWL 1.0 (see Section 3.2.1 on DL languages). RACERPRO comes with its own GUI named RACERPORTER.

---

[1] (Tsarkov and Horrocks 2006), http://owl.man.ac.uk/factplusplus/
[2] http://kaon2.semanticweb.org/
[3] (Sirin et al. 2007), http://pellet.owldl.com/
[4] (Haarslev and Möller 2003), http://www.racer-systems.com
[5] http://protege.stanford.edu/

3.2 DL Knowledge Bases

Knowledge is specified in a *knowledge base* (KB) in DL syntax. The KB comprises two components, the *TBox* and the *ABox*. The TBox introduces the *terminology*, i.e. a set of axioms that describes the application domain, while the ABox consists of *assertions* about particular *individuals* in terms of this vocabulary. A formal account of the TBox and ABox language constructs and their set-theoretic semantics is given in the following.

3.2.1 The TBox

Syntax of Descriptions

The TBox consists of a set of TBox axioms, which in turn contain *concept and role descriptions*. Descriptions are built inductively from *concept names* (like Road) and *role names* (like hasPart) using *constructors* (like "and" or "not"). Any concept or role name is also a trivial concept or role description respectively. Let C and D be concept descriptions, and r and s be role descriptions, then all terms given in the first two columns of Table 3.1 are concept and role descriptions as well.

According to this definition, the following two terms are examples of concept descriptions

> // *Roads which only have one-way lanes*
> Road ⊓ ∀hasPart.OneWayLane
> // *Lanes which have a right turn arrow*
> Lane ⊓ ∃hasPart.RightTurnArrow   ,

whereas the following terms are examples for role descriptions

> // *Individual pairs, which overlap but are not a part of each other*
> overlapsWith ⊓ ¬hasPart ⊓ ¬isPartOf
> // *Individual pairs, where the first component overlaps with*
> // *an object that has the second component as a part*
> overlapsWith ∘ hasPart   .

Additionally to the introduced role constructors, some further restrictions can be imposed on a role. It can be declared *functional*, which means that any individual is allowed maximally one role relation to another individual. hasMother is an

Table 3.1:

Syntax of concept and role descriptions		
Syntax	**Name**	**Language**
$\top$	Universal/Top concept	$\mathcal{AL}$
$\bot$	Bottom concept	$\mathcal{AL}$
$\neg C$	Negation	$\mathcal{C}$
$C \sqcap D$	Conjunction	$\mathcal{AL}$
$C \sqcup D$	Disjunction	$\mathcal{U}$
$\forall r.C$	Universal quantification	$\mathcal{AL}$
$\exists r.C$	Existential quantification	$\mathcal{E}$
$\exists_{\leq n} r.C$	Qualified min number restriction	$\mathcal{Q}$
$\exists_{\geq n} r.C$	Qualified max number restriction	$\mathcal{Q}$
$\exists_{=} r.C$	Qualified max number restriction	$\mathcal{Q}$
$r \doteq s$	Agreement (requires functional roles)	$\mathcal{F}$
$r \neq s$	Disagreement (requires functional roles)	$\mathcal{F}$
r^-	Role Inverse	$.^{-1}/\mathcal{I}$
$r \sqcap s$	Role Intersection	$.\sqcap$
$r \sqcup s$	Role Union	$.\sqcup$
$\neg r$	Role Complement	$.\neg$
$r \circ s$	Role Chain / Role Composition	$.\circ$
r^+	Transitive Role Closure	$.+$

example for a functional role. Roles can also be declared *symmetric*, *reflexive* and *transitive*, with the obvious semantics.

Some DL languages also allow for individual names in the TBox, which are then called *nominals*, as for example *TheRoadNetwork*. They are also called *singleton sets*.

Syntax of Axioms

The set of axioms that constitutes the TBox is constructed from the previously introduced concept and role descriptions according to Table 3.2. Inclusion axioms specify necessary conditions for concept membership. Equality axioms, by contrast, *define* a concept by formalising necessary and sufficient conditions. $C \equiv D$ is an abbreviation for mutual inclusion: $C \sqsubseteq D$ and $D \sqsubseteq C$.

3.2. DL KNOWLEDGE BASES

Table 3.2:

Syntax	Terminological Axioms	
	Name	Language
$C \sqsubseteq D$	(General) Concept inclusion / Implication	$\mathcal{AL}$
$C \equiv D$	Concept equality / Definition	$\mathcal{AL}$
$r \sqsubseteq s$	Role inclusion	$\mathcal{H}$

Example 3.1. A small example TBox is given by the following set of axioms:

$\mathcal{T} = \{$ // *A road can either be one-way or two-way.*
  Road $\equiv$ OneWayRoad $\sqcup$ TwoWayRoad ,
  // *Two-way roads are disjoint from one-way roads.*
  TwoWayRoad $\sqsubseteq \neg$OneWayRoad ,
  // *A road contains lanes only, and it contains at least one lane.*
  Road $\sqsubseteq \forall$hasPart.Lane $\sqcap \exists$hasPart.Lane ,
  // *A lane is either one-way or two-way.*
  Lane $\equiv$ OneWayLane $\sqcup$ TwoWayLane ,
  // *A one-way road contains one-way lanes only.*
  OneWayRoad $\sqsubseteq \forall$hasPart.OneWayLane ,
  // *A one-way road never contains a u-turn lane.*
  OneWayRoad $\sqsubseteq \forall$hasPart.$\neg$UTurnLane ,
  // *A lane containing a u-turn marking is a u-turn lane.*
  Lane $\sqcap \exists$hasPart.UTurnMarking $\sqsubseteq$ UTurnLane $\}$.

The last axiom is called a general inclusion axiom, as its left hand side contains a non-trivial description. The role hasPart is declared inverse of the role isPartOf (not shown in $\mathcal{T}$), which will be used later on. Both are not declared transitive, so they must be read as "has direct part" and "is direct part of".

If the fifth axiom was turned into a definition by using the $\equiv$-constructor, it would allow a OneWayRoad to contain one-way lanes with opposing driving directions, which does not capture the intuitive concept semantics. A reasonable definition of a OneWayRoad is

$\mathcal{T}_{Roads} = \mathcal{T} \cup \{$
    // A road is one-way iff it only consists of one-way lanes either all
    // pointing north, or all south (relative to the road coord. system).
    OneWayRoad ≡ Road ⊓ (∀hasPart.OneWayLaneNorth ⊔
                               ∀hasPart.OneWayLaneSouth) ,
    // A one-way lane is either pointing north or south.
    OneWayLane ≡ OneWayLaneNorth ⊔ OneWayLaneSouth ,
    // One-way lane north is disjoint from one-way lane south.
    OneWayLaneNorth ⊑ ¬OneWayLaneSouth $\}$.

The TBox $\mathcal{T}_{Roads}$ will be used for subsequent examples in this chapter. ∎

Using definitions, an individual which "meets" the description will automatically be classified as an instance of the defined concept.

DL Languages

The term Description Logic denotes a whole family of knowledge representation languages. A particular DL language is determined by the provided subset of constructors from Table 3.1, and its name is built through concatenation of the corresponding symbols given in the table's right column. Generally speaking, using more constructs in a language enhances its expressiveness but can jeopardise its decidability. A well studied, basic DL is $\mathcal{ALC}$, which only consists of conjunction, disjunction, universal quantification, a limited form of existential quantification, and negation. The letter $\mathcal{S}$ is used as an abbreviation for the language $\mathcal{ALC}_{R+}$, the subscript $\cdot_{R+}$ of which denotes the possibility of declaring transitive roles.

The DL used in this contribution is $\mathcal{ALCQHI}_{R+}$, or $\mathcal{SHIQ}$. It extends $\mathcal{ALC}_{R+}$ with role hierarchies, inverse roles, qualified number restrictions. It has been proven to be decidable in EXPTIME (Tobies 2001) and it is supported by the RACERPRO reasoner. For decidability reasons, qualified number restrictions are only allowed for so-called *simple roles* in this DL. Such roles are neither transitive themselves nor do they have a transitive subrole.

3.2.2 The ABox

The ABox captures knowledge about a specific state of affairs. It is formulated in terms of the vocabulary that is set up in the TBox. Syntactically, the ABox consists

3.2. DL KNOWLEDGE BASES

Table 3.3:

Assertional Axioms	
Syntax	**Name**
$a : \mathsf{C}$	Concept assertion
$(a, b) : \mathsf{r}$	Role assertion
$a = b$	Semantic Equality
$a \neq b$	Semantic Inequality

of a set of *assertions* about *individuals*. The four possible types of assertions are given in Table 3.3. Variables a and b denote individual names.

An individual a that satisfies a concept assertion $a : \mathsf{C}$ is also denoted an *instance* of C, or said to be *of type* C.

If a KR system follows the *open world assumption* (OWA) then the absence of information in the ABox indicates lack of knowledge. The closed world assumption (CWA) in contrast, which underlies database systems and Prolog, treats absence of information as negative information. DL adopts the OWA.

If a reasoner applies the *unique name assumption* (UNA), differently named individuals must never refer to identical domain elements. UNA can be switched on and off in RACERPRO.

Example 3.2. A small ABox for the TBox $\mathcal{T}_{Roads}$ from Example 3.1 is given by:

$\mathcal{A} = \{$ *georgeSt* : Road ,
    $(lane_{07}, georgeSt)$: isPartOf ,
    $(lane_{42}, georgeSt)$: isPartOf ,
    $arrow_{01}$: UTurnMarking ,
    $(arrow_{01}, lane_{42})$: isPartOf $\}$

The second individual in a role assertion is called the role *filler*: *georgeSt* is an isPartOf filler for individual $lane_{42}$.

Under CWA, from $\mathcal{A}$ and $\mathcal{T}_{Roads}$, it follows that

// George St. has maximally two lanes.
georgeSt: $\exists_{\leq 2}$ hasPart.Lane ,

as only two fillers of the role hasPart were explicitly asserted, whereas under OWA, the number of its lanes is unknown. This form of deductive reasoning is called entailment and will be introduced in detail in Section 3.3.2.3. When furthermore UNA is switched on under OWA, it also follows that

// George St. has at least two lanes.
$georgeSt : \exists_{\geq 2} \, hasPart.Lane$,

Without UNA, by contrast, the total number of lanes could also equal one, as it could additionally be the case that $lane_{42} = lane_{07}$ holds. ∎

3.2.3 Semantics

The semantics of axioms has so far only been hinted at by means of "speaking" names and comments. Next, a formal semantics for all types of axioms is provided using set theory. A precisely defined semantics is crucial for minimising the chance of semantic ambiguities in a knowledge base.

The semantics of concept and role descriptions is given through an *interpretation* $\mathcal{I}$. An interpretation consists of a non-empty set $\Delta^{\mathcal{I}}$, called the *domain* of $\mathcal{I}$, and an interpretation function. This function assigns to every concept name C a set $C^{\mathcal{I}} \subseteq \Delta^{\mathcal{I}}$ and to every role name r a binary relation $R^{\mathcal{I}} \subseteq \Delta^{\mathcal{I}} \times \Delta^{\mathcal{I}}$. The interpretation function is extended to concept and role descriptions according to Table 3.4.

An interpretation $\mathcal{I}$ *satisfies* a terminological or assertional axiom iff the respective condition in the table's right column is satisfied. An interpretation $\mathcal{I}$ is a *model* of a TBox $\mathcal{T}$ if all its terminological axioms are satisfied. $\mathcal{I}$ is a model of an ABox $\mathcal{A}$ with respect to $\mathcal{T}$, if it is a model of $\mathcal{T}$ and satisfies all axioms in $\mathcal{A}$.

Example 3.3. For $\mathcal{T}_{Roads}$ and $\mathcal{A}$ from Examples 3.1 - 3.2, one of many interpretations is:

$$
\begin{aligned}
\Delta^{\mathcal{I}} &= \{georgeSt, lane_{42}, lane_{07}, arrow_{01}\} \\
\text{Road}^{\mathcal{I}} &= \{georgeSt\} \\
\text{OneWayRoad}^{\mathcal{I}} &= \{\} \\
\text{TwoWayRoad}^{\mathcal{I}} &= \{georgeSt\} \\
\text{Lane}^{\mathcal{I}} &= \{lane_{42}, lane_{07}\} \\
\text{OneWayLane}^{\mathcal{I}} &= \{lane_{42}, lane_{07}\} \\
\text{TwoWayLane}^{\mathcal{I}} &= \{\} \\
\text{OneWayLaneSouth}^{\mathcal{I}} &= \{lane_{07}\} \\
\text{OneWayLaneNorth}^{\mathcal{I}} &= \{lane_{42}\} \\
\text{UTurnLane}^{\mathcal{I}} &= \{lane_{42}\} \\
\text{UTurnMarking}^{\mathcal{I}} &= \{arrow_{01}\}
\end{aligned}
$$

3.2. DL KNOWLEDGE BASES

Table 3.4:

Semantics of concept and role descriptions, satisfiability conditions for TBox axioms and ABox assertions

Syntax	Semantics
$\top$	$\Delta^\mathcal{I}$ for concepts, $\Delta^\mathcal{I} \times \Delta^\mathcal{I}$ for roles
$\bot$	$\emptyset$
$C \sqcap D$	$C^\mathcal{I} \cap D^\mathcal{I}$
$C \sqcup D$	$C^\mathcal{I} \cup D^\mathcal{I}$
$\neg C$	$\Delta^\mathcal{I} \setminus C^\mathcal{I}$
$\forall r.C$	$\{a \in \Delta^\mathcal{I} \mid \forall b \in \Delta^\mathcal{I} : (a,b) \in R^\mathcal{I} \Rightarrow b \in C^\mathcal{I}\}$
$\exists r.C$	$\{a \in \Delta^\mathcal{I} \mid \exists b \in \Delta^\mathcal{I} : (a,b) \in R^\mathcal{I} \land b \in C^\mathcal{I}\}$
$\exists_{\leq n} r.C$	$\{a \in \Delta^\mathcal{I} \mid \|\{x \mid (a,x) \in R^\mathcal{I}, x \in C^\mathcal{I}\}\| \leq n\}$
$\exists_{\geq n} r.C$	$\{a \in \Delta^\mathcal{I} \mid \|\{x \mid (a,x) \in R^\mathcal{I}, x \in C^\mathcal{I}\}\| \geq n\}$
$r \doteq s$	$\{a \in \Delta^\mathcal{I} \mid \exists b \in \Delta^\mathcal{I} : (a,b) \in R^\mathcal{I} \land (a,b) \in S^\mathcal{I}\}$
$r \not\doteq s$	$\{a \in \Delta^\mathcal{I} \mid \exists b_1, b_2 \in \Delta^\mathcal{I}, b_1 \neq b_2 : (a,b_1) \in R^\mathcal{I} \land (a,b_2) \in S^\mathcal{I}\}$
I	$I^\mathcal{I} \subseteq \Delta^\mathcal{I}$, with $|I^\mathcal{I}| = 1$
r^-	$\{(b,a) \in \Delta^\mathcal{I} \times \Delta^\mathcal{I} \mid (a,b) \in R^\mathcal{I}\}$
$r \sqcap s$	$R^\mathcal{I} \cap S^\mathcal{I}$
$r \sqcup s$	$R^\mathcal{I} \cup S^\mathcal{I}$
$\neg r$	$\Delta^\mathcal{I} \times \Delta^\mathcal{I} \setminus R^\mathcal{I}$
$r \circ s$	$R^\mathcal{I} \circ S^\mathcal{I}$
r^+	$\bigcup_{n \geq 1} (R^\mathcal{I})^n$
$C \sqsubseteq D$	$C^\mathcal{I} \subseteq D^\mathcal{I}$
$C \equiv D$	$C^\mathcal{I} = D^\mathcal{I}$
$r \sqsubseteq s$	$R^\mathcal{I} \subseteq S^\mathcal{I}$
$a : C$	$a^\mathcal{I} \in C^\mathcal{I}$
$(a,b) : r$	$(a^\mathcal{I}, b^\mathcal{I}) \in R^\mathcal{I}$
$a = b$	$a^\mathcal{I} = b^\mathcal{I}$
$a \neq b$	$a^\mathcal{I} \neq b^\mathcal{I}$

$$\text{hasPart}^{\mathcal{I}} = \{(georgeSt, lane_{07}), (georgeSt, lane_{42}), (lane_{42}, arrow_{01})\}$$
$$\text{isPartOf}^{\mathcal{I}} = \{(lane_{07}, georgeSt), (lane_{42}, georgeSt), (arrow_{01}, lane_{42})\}$$

This interpretation is also a model of $\mathcal{T}$ and $\mathcal{A}$, as all terminological and assertional axioms are satisfied. ∎

3.3 DL Inference Services

The purpose of a DL-based KR system goes beyond mere storage of data. Its formal semantics make it possible to explicate knowledge, which is only implicitly contained in the data, by means of inference steps. This type of inference is called *deduction*. Looking at mathematics, theorem proving from a set of axioms is an example of deductive reasoning. In DL, deductive reasoning can be divided into TBox and ABox inference. TBox inference is useful during terminological modelling of the application domain, to test whether the declared concepts "make sense". ABox inference is usually employed during usage of the knowledge base within an application. It is used there to test the input data for consistency, to pose boolean queries to the KB, and to retrieve tuples of individuals, among which a specified set of conditions must hold. The amount of inference services implemented in modern KR systems varies, and, in particular, optimised ABox reasoning is not provided by all systems.

3.3.1 TBox Inference

Subsumption

A concept D *subsumes* a concept C with respect to a TBox $\mathcal{T}$ iff $\mathsf{C}^{\mathcal{I}} \subseteq \mathsf{D}^{\mathcal{I}}$ holds for each model $\mathcal{I}$. This is written as $\mathcal{T} \models \mathsf{C} \sqsubseteq \mathsf{D}$. The operator $\models$ is called the *entailment* operator.

Example 3.4. As a simple example, in $\mathcal{T}_{Roads}$ from Example 3.1, $\mathcal{T}_{Roads} \models$ OneWayRoad $\sqsubseteq$ Road. From a given set of TBox axioms, all modern reasoners can automatically infer the concept subsumption hierarchy or *taxonomy*. Figure 3.2 shows the subsumption hierarchy which results from $\mathcal{T}_{Roads}$.

3.3. DL INFERENCE SERVICES

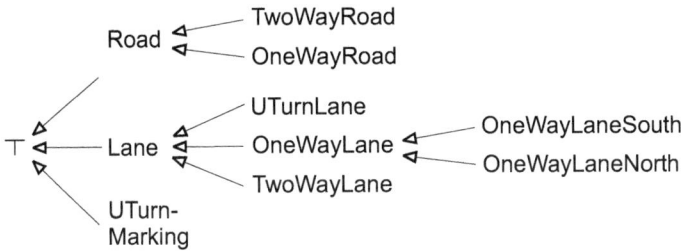

Figure 3.2: Subsumption Hierarchy / Taxonomy. ∎

Satisfiability

A concept C is called *satisfiable* with respect to a TBox $\mathcal{T}$ iff there is a model $\mathcal{I}$ of $\mathcal{T}$ where $C^{\mathcal{I}} \neq \emptyset$. Otherwise the concept is called *unsatisfiable*. A TBox $\mathcal{T}$ is satisfiable if there exists a model of $\mathcal{T}$. A satisfiable TBox is also called *coherent*. Satisfiability can be reduced to the subsumption problem: A concept C is called *unsatisfiable* with respect to a TBox $\mathcal{T}$ iff $\mathcal{T} \models C \sqsubseteq \bot$. Usually, an unsatisfiable TBox indicates an error in domain modelling, as it contains a concept which by definition cannot have any instances.

Example 3.5. The TBox $\mathcal{T}_{Roads}$ is satisfiable, as a model was already provided in Example 3.3. However, when adding the axiom

$$\text{MixedRoad} \equiv \text{OneWayRoad} \sqcap \text{TwoWayRoad} , \tag{3.1}$$

then $\mathcal{T}_{Roads}$ becomes unsatisfiable, as it contains the conjunction of two disjoint concepts, which is always subsumed by the empty set. ∎

Disjointness

Two concepts C and D are disjoint iff $C^{\mathcal{I}} \cap D^{\mathcal{I}} = \emptyset$ holds for each model $\mathcal{I}$. Disjointness can as well be reduced to subsumption: Two concepts C and D are disjoint iff $C \sqcap D$ is subsumed by $\bot$.

3.3.2 ABox Inference

3.3.2.1 Consistency

An ABox $\mathcal{A}$ is *consistent* with respect to $\mathcal{T}$, iff there exists a model of $\mathcal{T}$ and $\mathcal{A}$. Otherwise the ABox is called *inconsistent*. An inconsistent ABox indicates that the input data violates at least one domain model assumption. In deduction, false premises can lead to false conclusions, therefore an inconsistent ABox will generally not produce correct reasoning results. In a consistent TBox, consistency checking is used to detect erroneous input data (with respect to $\mathcal{T}$).

Example 3.6. The ABox $\mathcal{A}$ defined in Example 3.2 is obviously consistent, because a model has been given in Example 3.3. But when adding the axiom

$\qquad georgeSt : \textsf{OneWayRoad}\quad,$

the ABox will become inconsistent with respect to $\mathcal{T}_{Roads}$, as by definition, u-turn lanes must not occur on a one-way road. ∎

3.3.2.2 Instance Classification/Realisation Problem

Realisation or instance classification denotes the inference service, which, given an individual i in $\mathcal{A}$, returns the most specific set of concepts of which i is an instance.

Example 3.7. Again referring to $\mathcal{T}_{Roads}$ and $\mathcal{A}$ from Example 3.2, then instance classification yields

$\qquad i = georgeSt\ :\ \{\textsf{TwoWayRoad}\}$
$\qquad i = lane_{42}\quad\ :\ \{\textsf{UTurnLane}\}\quad.$

A less trivial TBox might return more than one concept name per individual. ∎

The additionally inferred assertions can usually be chosen to be automatically added to the ABox by the reasoner. Such an augmented ABox is termed *realised*.

3.3.2.3 Instance Checking

Instance checking tests whether an assertion is *entailed* by a KB, written $\mathcal{KB} \models \alpha$. An ABox assertion α is entailed by $\mathcal{KB}$, iff every model of $\mathcal{KB}$ also satisfies α. If α is a concept assertion $a : \textsf{C}$, and $\mathcal{KB}$ is known to be consistent, then instance checking can be reduced to testing the consistency of $\mathcal{KB} \cup \{a : \neg\textsf{C}\}$.

Example 3.8. As an example, the assertion

$\qquad$// *George St. has some lane with driving direction southwards.*
$\qquad \alpha = \{georgeSt : \exists\textsf{hasPart}.(\textsf{OneWayLaneSouth} \sqcup \textsf{TwoWayLane})\}$

3.3. DL INFERENCE SERVICES

is entailed by the above KB, even though neither a one-way lane pointing southwards nor a two-way lane have been asserted for George St. This is because George St. is two-way, which has been axiomatised as not one-way, which is defined implicitly from the given axioms as

// A road is a two-way road, iff it contains
// a one-way lane pointing northwards and one pointing southwards,
// or if it contains a two-way lane.
TwoWayRoad ≡ Road ⊓ (
    (∃hasPart.OneWayLaneNorth ⊓
      ∃hasPart.OneWayLaneSouth) ⊔
    ∃hasPart.TwoWayLane)   ∎

3.3.2.4 Retrieval and Conjunctive Queries

Given a concept description C, a retrieval query returns all individuals i which are instances of C, i.e. for which $\mathcal{KB} \models i{:}\mathsf{C}$ holds. Conjunctive retrieval querying is more general than retrieval: It returns all tuples of individuals $(i_1, \ldots, i_n)$ among which a set of conditions holds. These conditions are formulated through query terms q of the form $x_i : \mathsf{C}$ or $(x_i, x_j) : \mathsf{r}$, where x_i, x_j are either variables or individual names. A conjunctive retrieval query is of the form

$$\underbrace{(x_1, \ldots, x_n)}_{\text{query head}} \leftarrow \underbrace{q_1 \wedge \cdots \wedge q_n}_{\text{query body}}$$

The answer to a retrieval query Q with respect to a KB is the set of tuples of individual names $(i_1, \ldots, i_n)$ occurring in the KB, such that, by substituting $(i_1, \ldots, i_n)$ for $(x_1, \ldots, x_n)$ in the query terms of Q, the assertions in the grounded query terms are a logical consequence of the KB.

Example 3.9. The query

$$(x_1, x_2) \leftarrow x_1 : \mathsf{Road} \wedge (x_1, x2) : \mathsf{hasPart} \wedge x_2 : \mathsf{UTurnLane}$$

returns all roads and their u-turn lanes. In the case of $\mathcal{T}_{Roads}$ and ABox $\mathcal{A}$ only the tuple

$$\{(georgeSt, lane_{42})\}$$

is returned.   ∎

Retrieval queries are widely known from databases, where SQL is the dominant query language. There, retrieving instances reduces to simple model checking. In DL no single minimal model can be computed, as, in general, a DLKB will be nondeterministic (due to the $\exists$ and the $\sqcup$ constructors) and incomplete (due to the OWA (cf. Section 3.2.1)). Therefore, deductive reasoning is needed when answering a query in a DL setting.

3.4 Rules

In some cases it is desirable to relate more than two ABox individuals. In full FOL, this is easily achieved using predicates of arity greater than two. As DL is a fragment of FOL restricted to unary and binary predicates, relating three or more individuals requires so-called *role chains*, which are composition of role names written as $r_1 \circ \cdots \circ r_n$, and a concept constructor called *role-value-map*, which is written as $r \sqsubseteq s$ for two role chains r and s (see the following Example 3.10). However, (Schmidt-Schauß 1989) have shown that role-value-maps make reasoning undecidable already for a language as simple as $\mathcal{ALC}$.

To overcome the resulting limitations in expressivity (and also for other reasons), current research points towards an integration of DL-based and *rule-based representation formalisms*, which originate from Logic Programming (e. g. (Horrocks and Patel-Schneider 2004)). The following description of rule syntax and semantics refers to a pragmatic ABox augmentation using *trigger rules*[6] which is supported by the RACERPRO reasoner since version 1.9.

Rules consist of a body and a head:

$$\underbrace{r_1 \wedge \cdots \wedge r_m}_{\text{rule head (consequence)}} \leftarrow \underbrace{q_1 \wedge \cdots \wedge q_n}_{\text{rule body (antecedent)}} .$$

The syntax of the rule terms q_i and r_j is equivalent to that of the query terms defined in the previous section, with the restriction that only those variable names which are mentioned in the rule body are allowed in the rule head.

The semantics of a rule-enhanced KB can be defined by a forward-chaining reasoning process: A rule *fires*, if a set of individual names can be assigned to the set of its variables so that each assertion in its body is a logical consequence of the KB. The assertions contained in its grounded rule consequence are then added to the ABox. In this manner, rule consequences are added to an ABox until no more rules can fire. This process eventually halts as a KB contains only finitely many

---

[6]The terms *trigger rules* and *rules* will be used synonymously in the following.

3.4. Rules

individuals and finitely many rules. Because of the monotonicity of DL reasoning (adding new assertions can never make previously asserted or inferred assertions invalid), if the rules are also monotonic in nature, this process is independent of the order of rule application[7]. The resulting augmented KB is called the *procedural extension* of the initial KB.

Example 3.10. Let hasNeighbour denote a role which relates two adjacent lanes within a road. In DL, capturing the notion that neighbouring lanes must be part of the *same* road would require an axiom containing a role-value map of the form

// Roads must contain lanes, and the set of lanes is equal
// to set of the neighbours of these lanes.
Road $\sqsubseteq$ $\exists$hasPart.Lane $\sqcap$
 (hasPart $\circ$ hasNeighbour $\dot{\sqsubseteq}$ hasPart) ,

leading to undecidability. By contrast, this fact can easily be expressed using a rule:

(x_3, x_1) : isPartOf $\Leftarrow$
x_1 : Road $\wedge$ (x_2, x_1) : isPartOf $\wedge$ (x_2, x_3) : hasNeighbour .

∎

Although seemingly identical, there is a subtle difference in semantics between a rule of the form x : Road $\leftarrow$ x : OneWayRoad and a simple inclusion axiom OneWayRoad $\sqsubseteq$ Road. For the inclusion axiom, the *law of contraposition* holds, i.e. ¬Road $\sqsubseteq$ ¬OneWayRoad is entailed by the above axiom. This is not true for the corresponding rule, where no statement whatsoever is made about individuals which are *not* of type OneWayRoad. This type of trigger rules thus exclusively operates on ABoxes.

---

[7] As an example for a non-monotonic rule, consider a rule language allowing for the negation-as-failure operator ('neg'), which is true iff the truth value of its argument *cannot be proven wrong*. By contrast, classical negation ('¬') is true iff its argument *is provably wrong*. Apparently, the firing of a non-monotonic rule is dependant on whether the assertion contained in its argument is made before or after rule execution.

4 DL Formalisation of Scene Understanding

Modularity and reusability are major motivations behind the use of declarative, logic-based knowledge specifications. Unfortunately, reusable KBs and substantial literature on KB engineering do not yet exist for logic-based Computer Vision. Their accessability, however, is crucial for benefiting from these hoped-for properties.

This chapter makes one step in this direction, by elaborating on the mapping of several classic Computer Vision issues to a DL setting. Section 4.1 treats the incorporation of various classes of input data from an external sensor into a formal logic KB. Section 4.2 elaborates on the specification of qualitative scene geometry models in DL. Section 4.3 describes how several classical problems within Scene Understanding can be solved by DL inference services. In particular, object detection and classification, link prediction and data association are covered.

Implementations will be provided in the form of *design patterns*. A design pattern proposes a representation for a particular class of problems. It comprises a *template*, a generic code fragment in DL, which can be instantiated by a domain modeler for his or her particular task. A template will be indicated by an underscore, like $\mathcal{KB}_{MY\_TEMPLATE}$, its instantiation will omit the underscore, $\mathcal{KB}_{MY TEMPLATE}$. Within a template, all concepts, roles, or individuals requiring instantiation will also be indicated by an underscore, $\underline{C}, \underline{r}$ and $\underline{i}$, respectively. All KB design patterns use the decidable DL $\mathcal{SHIQ}$ (cf. Section 3.2.1 for the nomenclature for DL languages), which is also supported by the RACERPRO system.

The KB modelling principles introduced here form the basis for the Intersection Understanding KB presented in Chapter 5.

4.1 Formalisation of Data Input

In a Scene Interpretation system, external sensors acquire evidence about a particular scene. The characteristics of such input data can vary along several axes: 1. Is the number of scene objects known a priori or not? 2. Is the input data *partial* or *complete*? 3. Does the sensing algorithm deliver *sets of features (cues)* or *objects*? 4. Is only a *single* sensor or a *distributed* set of sensors involved? 5. For sensor sets: Is the setup *complementary* or *redundant*?[1] In the most general Scene Interpretation setup, the number of objects will be unknown, the input data will be globally incomplete, but complete within certain subsets, and the sensor setup will include both complementary and redundant sensors.

Subsection 4.1.1 shows that, in the Scene Interpretation context, DL's KR paradigms correspond to a partial number of objects and partial information about those objects. Completeness of data, on the other hand, is not representable. Therefore a design pattern, which approximates local completeness via a procedural extension to the KB, will be provided. Subsection 4.1.2 shows that complementary as well as redundant sensor data, and feature as well as object input, are representable in DL. A design pattern for each of these setups will be provided.

4.1.1 Partial vs. Complete Data

Open World Assumption vs. Closed World Assumption

KR formalisms adopting a *Closed World Assumption (CWA)*, like database systems or Prolog, treat absence of information as negative information (see Sec. 3.2.1):

$$\text{If } \mathcal{KB} \not\models \alpha \text{ then } \mathcal{KB} \models \neg\alpha \quad ,$$

where α is an assertion. Consequently, under CWA, the truth values "false" and "unknown" cannot be distinguished. As elaborated in Chapter 1, visual evidence is typically highly partial, and thus CWA semantics is not appropriate for Scene Interpretation. It instead requires an *Open World Assumption (OWA)*, where information is considered partial by default and no truth value is deduced for absent information. As a fragment of FOL, the DL family of KR formalisms inherits the OWA.

A KB interpreted under OWA inherently allows for *multiple models* (cf. 3.2.3). The set of models corresponds to the set of Scene Interpretation hypotheses that is consistent with the background knowledge and the partial sensor data. The more sensor data is available, the smaller the number of models gets.

The usage of an OWA-based KR formalism bears the problem that not even local completeness of information is expressible any more. The next but one paragraph will sketch why this is problematic for certain Scene Interpretation cases, and an

---

[1] A further relevant characteristic of sensor data is *data uncertainty*. For reasons explained in Section 1.3.2 this aspect is outside the scope of this thesis.

4.1. FORMALISATION OF DATA INPUT

approximation to a special case of local CWA will be given in the form of a procedural KB extension.

Open Domain vs. Closed Domain

Under a *closed domain assumption*, all individuals are known to the KB a priori:

$$\top \sqsubseteq \{i_1, i_2, \ldots, i_n\} \quad ,$$

where $\{i_1, i_2, \ldots, i_n\}$ is the set of individual names in the ABox. In a Scene Interpretation context this amounts to assuming that all relevant scene objects are known. With respect to the task of image segmentation, for example, it means that a complete low-level segmentation is provided initially. Typically, however, the detected set of objects will be incomplete due to occlusions, imperfect sensors and a limited field of view, and therefore new individuals need to be hypothesised by a combination of bottom-up and top-down reasoning. Scene Interpretation thus requires an *open domain* view, which is inherent to DL languages.

However, (at least) the following issues require special treatment in an open domain: Although existence of further individuals can be implied in a DLKB through the existential quantifier (e. g.: RightTurnLane $\sqsubseteq$ $\exists$hasPart.RightTurnArrow), the explicit construction of new individuals is outside the scope of classic DL reasoning. To enable hypothesisation of new individuals, either the pre-introduction of all potential scene objects or non-classic DL reasoning is required. These topics will be further elaborated in Section 4.3 on DL reasoning for Scene Interpretation.

Local Closures

Even though an open world and an open domain view are indispensable, a KR formalism for Scene Interpretation must nevertheless be capable of interpreting certain subsets of the provided KB information as being *locally complete*:

Example 4.1. In an ABox $\mathcal{A}$, evidence for a junction is given in the form of data from a topological map and from a vision sensor: $\mathcal{A} = \mathcal{A}_{map} \cup \mathcal{A}_{camera}$. The topological map provides the complete set of roads for a given junction[2]:

$$\mathcal{A}_{map} = \{\ junction_{01} : \text{Junction} \qquad , \\
road_{01} : \text{Road},\ road_{02} : \text{Road},\ road_{03} : \text{Road}\ , \\
(junction_{01}, road_{01}) : \text{hasPart} \qquad , \\
(junction_{01}, road_{02}) : \text{hasPart} \qquad , \\
(junction_{01}, road_{03}) : \text{hasPart} \qquad \}\ ,$$

---
[2]This example adopts the unique name assumption

i. e. $junction_{01}$ consists of three roads. The vision sensor has additionally detected an arrow marking on $road_{02}$:

$$\mathcal{A}_{vision} = \{\ (road_{02}, arrow_{01}) : \text{hasPart}\ \}\ .$$

The intended semantics behind these two specifications differs. Whereas the information provided in $\mathcal{A}_{vision}$ is partial (many more arrows may be present in the scene), the information in $\mathcal{A}_{map}$ is complete (the junction consists of exactly three roads). The intended meaning of $\mathcal{A}_{vision}$ is captured correctly due to DL's open world semantics, while the meaning of $\mathcal{A}_{map}$ is not, as the KB will allow all models where $junction_{01}$ has three *or more* roads. More particularly, using the TBox

$$\mathcal{T} = \{\ \text{ThreeBranchJunction} \equiv \text{Junction} \sqcap \exists_{=3}\text{hasPart.Road}\ \}$$

will not result in $junction_{01}$ being classified as a **ThreeBranchJunction** in $\mathcal{KB} = (\mathcal{T}, \mathcal{A})$, because more roads than the introduced ones might exist. ∎

A knowledge representation formalism for Scene Interpretation should therefore, while principally adopting the OWA, provide constructs to axiomatise that information given in the ABox is locally complete, i. e. make a *local closed world assumption* (LCWA) (Etzioni et al. 1994). A DL concept or role description **A** interpreted under LCWA allows only for those models in which **A** holds only for individuals or individual pairs for which **A** is implied by the KB. (Rosati 1998) axiomatises LCWA by using concept and role *closures*. Unfortunately, closures cannot yet be axiomatised in state of the art DL languages, but require an extension towards autoepistemic DL or circumscriptive DL (see e. g. (Grimm and Hitzler 2008)), or a combination of DL with Logic Programming (see e. g. (Motik et al. 2006)), all of which are subject of ongoing research. Next, an axiomatisation of LCWA for a special case termed *named atomic closure* is proposed. It will be approximated using available DL technology via a procedural extension to the KB.

Named Atomic Closure

Named atomic concept closure of an atomic concept **C** denotes that membership to **C** is interpreted under closed-world semantics for all named individuals i in the ABox $\mathcal{A}$ of a knowledge base $\mathcal{KB} = (\mathcal{T}, \mathcal{A})$:

If $\mathcal{KB} \not\models i : \textbf{C}$, then $\mathcal{KB} \models i : \neg\textbf{C}\ .$

In other words, a model of $\mathcal{KB}$ requires membership to **C** to hold exclusively for individuals, for which this fact is already implied by $\mathcal{KB}$'s axioms. All other

4.1. FORMALISATION OF DATA INPUT

individuals are instances of $\neg C$. An even stronger restriction will be termed *named told atomic concept closure*:

If $\mathcal{A} \not\models i : C$, then $\mathcal{KB} \models i : \neg C$.

Here a model of $\mathcal{KB}$ requires concept membership for an individual to hold exclusively if this has been *explicitly* asserted in the ABox.

Named atomic role closure of an atomic role r denotes, that r is interpreted under closed-world semantics for all named individual pairs (i,j) in the ABox:

If $\mathcal{KB} \not\models (i,j) : r$, then $\mathcal{KB} \models (i,j) : \neg r$.

Correspondingly, for *named told atomic role closure*:

If $\mathcal{A} \not\models (i,j) : r$, then $\mathcal{KB} \models (i,j) : \neg r$.

Provided that the named atomic closure semantics could be implemented, then in Example 4.1, either concept closure for Road or role closure of hasPart would achieve the desired reasoning results.

At least in principle, the semantics of named atomic concept closure could be approximated through a set of TBox *local domain closure axioms*:

$C \equiv \{c_1, \ldots, c_n\}$,

where $\{c_1, \ldots, c_n\}$ is the set of all individuals for which the assertion $c_i : C$ is implied by the KB. For Example 4.1, this would instantiate as Road $\equiv$ $\{road_{01}, road_{02}, road_{03}\}$. However, this axiomatisation involves nominals, the use of which considerably increases the complexity of reasoning. Only recently, (Horrocks and Sattler 2007) have proposed a tableau algorithm for the language $\mathcal{SHOIQ}$, which extends $\mathcal{SHIQ}$ by nominals, that is likely to perform well for ontologies of realistic size. It is not yet implemented in the RACERPRO system.

To conclude, not even the special cases of LCWA introduced here can be realised with currently available DL technology, nor can they be approximated by rules.

Approximation to Named Atomic Closure

At least on the assertional level, an approximation to the intended semantics can be achieved in $\mathcal{SHIQ}$ by using qualified number restrictions. This will be sketched for the case of role closures in the following.

First consider the following ABox enhancement: For any role r to be interpreted under named told closure semantics r, one max. number restriction is added for each ABox individual ind_i. Additionally, to prepare for later automation, each such role will be tagged as a descendant of closedWorldRole:

$\underline{r} \sqsubseteq$ closedWorldRole
$\underline{ind_1} : \exists_{\leq n_{R_1}}\underline{r}$
...
$\underline{ind_m} : \exists_{\leq n_{R_m}}\underline{r}$,

where n_{R_i} is the number of individuals which are explicitly asserted as fillers of role r for individual ind_i. This results in m axioms per closedWorldRole descendent. This ABox enhancement suffices to express the desired semantics in Example 4.1. However, it also prevents declaration of any further road parts detected by the vision sensor (e. g.: d_{01} : Divider, $(road_{03}, d_{01})$: hasPart). Therefore, r should only be *partially* closed with respect to particular concepts. The design pattern to achieve partial named closure for atomic role r reads as follows:

Pattern LOCALLY_CLOSED_WORLD:

Effect: Close role $\underline{r}$ with respect to fillers $\underline{C_1}, \ldots, \underline{C_k}$ for all individuals that are explicitly named in the ABox

Parameters:
- $\underline{r}$ — Atomic role
- $\underline{C_1}, \ldots, \underline{C_k}$ — Atomic concepts
- $\underline{ind_1}, \ldots, \underline{ind_m}$ — Complete set of named ABox individuals
- $n_{r_1}, \ldots, n_{r_m}$ — Number of $\underline{r}$-fillers of type $\underline{C_1} \sqcup \ldots \sqcup \underline{C_k}$ for individuals $\underline{ind_1}, \ldots, \underline{ind_m}$ respectively

Template:

$\mathcal{T}_{LOCALLY\_CLOSED\_WORLD} = \{$
  $\underline{r} \sqsubseteq$ closedWorldRole ,
  $\underline{C_1} \sqsubseteq$ ClosedWorldConcept ,
  ...
  $\underline{C_k} \sqsubseteq$ ClosedWorldConcept $\}$

$\mathcal{A}_{LOCALLY\_CLOSED\_WORLD} = \{$
  $\underline{ind_1} : \exists_{\leq n_{r_1}}\underline{r}.$ClosedWorldConcept ,
  ...
  $\underline{ind_m} : \exists_{\leq n_{r_m}}\underline{r}.$ClosedWorldConcept $\}$

Adding any more ClosedWorldConcept individuals as fillers of a

4.1. FORMALISATION OF DATA INPUT

closedWorldRole will now result in an ABox inconsistency. An example will illustrate more intuitively the effect of this pattern.

Example 4.2. To axiomatise that the list of Roads, which are part of $junction_{01}$ from Example 4.1, is complete, TBox and ABox Templates $\mathcal{T}_{LOCALLY\_CLOSED\_WORLD}$ and $\mathcal{A}_{LOCALLY\_CLOSED\_WORLD}$ must be instantiated as follows:

$\mathcal{T}_{LOCALLY\_CLOSED\_WORLD} = \{$
  hasPart $\sqsubseteq$ closedWorldRole ,
  Road $\sqsubseteq$ ClosedWorldConcept $\}$

$\mathcal{A}_{LOCALLY\_CLOSED\_WORLD} = \{$
  $junction_{01}$: $\exists_{\leq 3}$hasPart.ClosedWorldConcept ,
  $road_{01}$: $\exists_{\leq 0}$hasPart.ClosedWorldConcept ,
  $road_{02}$: $\exists_{\leq 0}$hasPart.ClosedWorldConcept ,
  $road_{03}$: $\exists_{\leq 0}$hasPart.ClosedWorldConcept ,
  $arrow_{01}$: $\exists_{\leq 0}$hasPart.ClosedWorldConcept $\}$.

Classification of the $\mathcal{KB}$ from Example 4.1 in union with $\mathcal{T}_{LOCALLY\_CLOSED\_WORLD}$ and $\mathcal{A}_{LOCALLY\_CLOSED\_WORLD}$ yields the desired result, namely: $\mathcal{KB} \models junction_{01}$: ThreeBranchJunction. ∎

Note that the above approximation requires knowledge of the cardinalities n_{r_i}. They are readily accessible (by counting) under UNA, or under non-UNA if the number of synonym ClosedWorldConcept individuals is known. For an unknown number of synonyms, although the ABox will remain consistent (due to usage of the "$\exists_{\leq}$"- instead of the "$\exists_{=}$"-constructor), role closure cannot be approximated by the above template.

Automatic ABox Augmentation by Closures

The manual provision of closure assertions to a KB as sketched in Template $\mathcal{A}_{LOCALLY\_CLOSED\_WORLD}$ can be automated within RACERPRO by using an extension of its query language nRQL called MiniLisp. MiniLisp is a simple expression language with which, among other things, aggregation operators (count, sum, average, ...) can be realised. The MiniLisp function (fire-closure-rules r C), which can be downloaded from the webpage given in the introductory chapter, automatically enhances a realised knowledge base with partial named role closure assertions with respect to atomic role r and fillers of atomic concept C. After declaration of that function, the following procedural extension yields KB closure as defined above for any KB implementing Template $\mathcal{T}_{LOCALLY\_CLOSED\_WORLD}$.

Algorithm 1 Named atomic closure for descendants of closedWorldRole

```
(full-reset)
(include-kb filename)
(realize-ABox)
(evaluate (fire-closure-rules 'closedWorldRole
    'ClosedWorldConcept))
```

By calling (fire-closure-rules) *before* ABox realization, a *told* closure semantics can alternatively be achieved.

4.1.2 Single vs. Distributed Sensor Setup

If only a still image acquired by a single sensor is interpreted on the object level, the unique name assumption (UNA, cf. Sec. 3.2.1) should be imposed. Intuitively spoken, it disallows synonym individual names in the ABox, and thus causes two individuals (like $object_{38}$ and $object_{35}$) to always be interpreted as different objects. UNA can be switched on in RACER by

(set-unique-name-assumption t) .

This case changes if data is acquired by multiple, non-complementary sensors, or if single-sensor data is accumulated over time. For overlapping fields of view, scene elements then become multiply detected. A typical scenario in the automotive context is data acquisition by an in-vehicle camera with a standard frame rate of around 20Hz. In another scenario, a fleet of vehicles equipped with external sensors approaches the same junction from different directions. The resulting detection redundancy in these scenarios is usually desired in order to reduce the false detection rate, and *data association* techniques are typically applied subsequently. In such cases, UNA must not be used. Nevertheless, semantic inequality between two particular individuals ind_i and ind_j should be axiomatised whenever reasonable. First, this rules out all models where ind_i and ind_j are synonyms. Second, UNA is often mistaken for granted by knowledge engineers, consequently leading to counterintuitive reasoning. Semantic inequality under non-UNA is axiomatised by the inequality constructor $ind_i \neq ind_j$ (cf. Table 3.3). As manual provision of these axioms is tedious and error-prone, this process should be automated.

Different classes of multi-sensor setups require different sets of inequality assertions. Subsequently, an automatic provision of the required inequality axioms is sketched for the four classes of sensor setups of *redundant* vs. *complementary* sensors and *set of features* vs. *object* level data input.

4.1. FORMALISATION OF DATA INPUT 51

Example 4.3 (Sensor setup: Redundant sensors, object level input). Following Example 4.1, a topological map provides a set of roads which are part of a junction.

$$\mathcal{A}_{map} = \{\ junction_{01} : \textsf{Junction} \ ,$$
$$road_{01} : \textsf{Road},\ road_{02} : \textsf{Road},\ road_{03} : \textsf{Road}\ ,$$
$$(junction_{01}, road_{01}) : \textsf{hasPart} \ ,$$
$$(junction_{01}, road_{02}) : \textsf{hasPart} \ ,$$
$$(junction_{01}, road_{03}) : \textsf{hasPart} \qquad\qquad \} \ .$$

This time, the vision sensor detects its own road, and two arrow markings on it:

$$\mathcal{A}_{vision} = \{\ egoroad : \textsf{Road},\ arrow_{01} : \textsf{Arrow},\ arrow_{02} : \textsf{Arrow}\ ,$$
$$(egoroad, arrow_{01}) : \textsf{hasPart} \ ,$$
$$(egoroad, arrow_{02}) : \textsf{hasPart} \qquad\qquad \} \ .$$

Apparently, the multi sensor setup is *redundant*: Consider a vehicle approaching $junction_{01}$, then semantic equality holds between the ego road and exactly one of $\mathcal{A}_{map}$'s roads,

$$\mathcal{KB} \models egoroad = road_{01} \lor egoroad = road_{02} \lor egoroad = road_{03} \ ,$$

and consequently UNA must not be used.

The input data is characterised by delivering data on an *object level* (in contrast to, e.g., descriptor-based object detectors like SIFT (Lowe 2004), which deliver sets of features). Therefore, pairwise inequality axioms must be added for the individuals within each ABox. Otherwise, under non-UNA, $junction_{01}$ will not classify as ThreeBranchJunction even after adding the closure axioms from Sec. 4.1.1, as some of the individual names might be synonyms. The same argumentation holds for the arrows in $\mathcal{A}_{vision}$.

In brief, for a redundant, object-based sensor setup, UNA must be replaced by a *local UNA* within each ABox part representing single sensor data. It is accounted for by partitioning the set of individual names according to the sensor image from which they were detected, and by axiomatising semantic inequality for each individual pair in each subset. The correct partition for this example is $\{\{junction_{01}, road_{01}, road_{02}, road_{03}\}, \{egoroad, arrow_{01}, arrow_{02}\}\}$. ∎

Each of the four sensor setups requires a different set of inequality assertions and thus a different partition of the set of individuals. The following design pattern tags the individuals in a KB according to the type of sensor setup being used[3]

---
[3]The constructor $\textsf{disjoint}(C_1, \ldots, C_n)$ is "syntactic sugar" for the set of axioms stating disjointness between each pair of arguments: $C_i \sqsubseteq \neg C_j\ \forall i, j \in 1, ..., n, i \neq j$. It is provided by most DL reasoners.

and provides the correct set of inequality assertions. The tagging will be used afterwards to provide the required assertions automatically through a procedural extension of the KB.

Pattern SENSOR_SETUP:

Effect: Provide correct set of inequality assertions for each of four sensor setups: redundant vs. complementary, objects vs. features.

Parameters: $\underline{\text{SensorInput}_1}, ..., \underline{\text{SensorInput}_n}$ Names of all sensors that provide ABox individuals
$\underline{ind_1}, ..., \underline{ind_m}$ Complete set of named ABox individuals

Template:

$\mathcal{T}_{SENSOR\_SETUP} = \{$
   SensorInput $\equiv \underline{\text{SensorInput}_1} \sqcup ... \sqcup \underline{\text{SensorInput}_n}$,
   // For each object-detecting sensor $i, i \in \{1, .., n\}$, add:
   $\underline{\text{SensorInput}_i} \sqsubseteq$ SceneObject   ,
   // For each set of complementary sensors add:
   disjoint($\underline{\text{SensorInput}_j}, ..., \underline{\text{SensorInput}_k}$)
$\}$

$\mathcal{A}_{SENSOR\_SETUP_1} = \{$
   $\underline{ind_1}$: $\underline{\text{SensorInput}_i}$,
   ...   ,
   $\underline{ind_m}$: $\underline{\text{SensorInput}_j}$ $\}$

$\mathcal{A}_{SENSOR\_SETUP_2} = \{$
   // For each $i \in \{1, .., n\}$:
   // For each individual pair (ind_j, ind_k) of type $SensorInput_i$:
   // If ind_j and ind_k are of type SceneObject add:
   $\underline{ind_j} \neq \underline{ind_k}$ $\}$

The concept name SensorInput refers to all individuals that are detected by a sensor. Individuals can either represent a scene object or a feature of a scene object. In the former case the individual is of type SceneObject. The concept names SensorInput and SceneObject will also be used in other design patterns. Pattern SENSOR_SETUP models each sensor as either a feature- or an object-delivering sensor. Furthermore, each pair of sensors is modelled as either complementary or redundant. $\mathcal{A}_{SENSOR\_SETUP_2}$ contains the appropriate disjointness assertions

4.1. FORMALISATION OF DATA INPUT

for each of the four sensor setups. The procedural KB extension described below provides these assertions automatically.

Example 4.4. For the above example, pattern SENSOR_SETUP instantiates as

$\mathcal{KB}_{SENSOR\_SETUP} = \{$
SensorInput $\equiv$ MapInput $\sqcup$ CameraInput ,
MapInput $\sqsubseteq$ SceneObject ,
CameraInput $\sqsubseteq$ SceneObject ,
$junction_{01}$: MapInput, ..., $road_{03}$: MapInput ,
$egoroad$: CameraInput, ..., $arrow_{02}$: CameraInput ,
$junction_{01} \neq road_{01}$, ..., $road_{02} \neq road_{03}$,
$egoroad \neq arrow_{01}$, ..., $arrow_{01} \neq arrow_{02}$
$\}$.

The precise characterisation of the sensor setup serves as the basis for *data association* reasoning (see Section 4.3.4).

Automatic ABox Enhancement by Local UNA

Calling the MiniLisp function (ensure-local-UNA 'SceneObject 'SensorInput) automatically enhances a KB containing $\mathcal{T}_{SENSOR\_SETUP}$ and $\mathcal{A}_{SENSOR\_SETUP_1}$ by $\mathcal{A}_{SENSOR\_SETUP_2}$. In other words, pairwise disjointness is asserted among all SceneObject individuals within each named subclass of SensorInput. The function can be downloaded from the web page given in the introductory chapter. Summarising the present and the last subsection, the following algorithm provides for a procedural extension of a KB that ensures local UNA for certain individual sets and named role closure for certain roles. The choice of individual sets and roles depends on the implementation of Templates $\mathcal{KB}_{SENSOR\_SETUP}$ and $\mathcal{KB}_{LOCALLY\_CLOSED\_WORLD}$.

Algorithm 2 Local UNA and named role closure

```
(full-reset)
(include-kb filename)
(evaluate(ensure-local-UNA 'SceneObject 'SensorInput))
(realize-ABox)
(evaluate(fire-closure-rules 'closedWorldRole
    'closedWorldConcept))
```

The user must assign a SensorInput class to each introduced individual. This is enforced be supplementing the instantiated template by the following rule:

$$x_1 : \bot \Leftarrow \text{neg}(x_1 : \text{SensorInput}) \ .$$

The neg-operator hereby denotes negation-as-failure (cf. Sec. 3.4) and is provided for trigger rules in the RACER system. It asserts the unsatisfiable concept $\bot$ to all those individuals, for which membership in SensorInput cannot be proven, resulting in an inconsistent ABox.

4.2 Modelling of Scene Geometry

This section elaborates on a principled procedure of modelling a hypothesis space of qualitative scene geometries for some particular class of scenes (such as intersections).

The hypothesis space proposed here is composed of two main components: A discrete set of geometries for each object, and a discrete set of spatial relations between each pair of objects. Modelling scene geometry can be viewed as imposing restrictions on the admissible object geometries and on the admissible spatial relations.

Subsection 4.2.1 provides a design pattern for axiomatising object geometry models, and Subsection 4.2.2 describes how to axiomatise qualitative spatial relations. Subsection 4.2.3 uses those spatial relations to set up a hypothesis space for relational scene geometry.

4.2.1 Object Geometry

Any object that potentially is physically present in the scene, has some geometric shape. One possibility of modelling that shape is as a composition of instantiated geometric primitives. A geometric primitive by itself is generic, i. e. it will typically possess some quantitative parameters (e. g. pose, width). It should be left to the domain modeler whether he or she wants to model/infer geometry for a particular object class or not.

This shape model can be formalised using the following design pattern:

4.2. MODELLING OF SCENE GEOMETRY

> **Pattern OBJECT_GEOMETRY:**
>
> **Effect:** Define a geometric primitive as a discrete set of n mutually disjoint concepts called GP1, ..., GPn. Define a geometric entity as a primitive or a composition of primitives.
> **Parameter:** n   Number of geometric primitives modeled
> **Template:**
>
> $\mathcal{T}_{OBJECT\_GEOMETRY} = \{$
>   GeometricPrimitive $\equiv$ GP1 $\sqcup$ GP2 $\sqcup$ ... $\sqcup$ GP<u>n</u>   ,
>   disjoint(GP1, GP2, ..., GP<u>n</u>)   ,
>   GeometricEntity $\equiv$ GeometricPrimitive $\sqcup$
>   ($\exists$pp.GeometricPrimitive $\sqcap$
> $\forall$pp.GeometricPrimitive   ) ,
>   GeometricEntity $\sqsubseteq$ SceneObject $\}$

The role **pp** is an abbreviation for "proper part", and will be formally introduced in Section 4.2.2 on spatial relations. **GP** is a shortcut for geometric primitive. Any scene object concept <u>C</u> introduced in the KB, like **Road** or **TrafficSign**, for which qualitative geometry shall be modelled or inferred, must inherit from **GeometricEntity**:

   <u>C</u> $\sqsubseteq$ GeometricEntity   .

Without further constraints, this allows instances of <u>C</u> to be composed of arbitrary combinations of geometric primitives. Using Pattern OBJECT_GEOMETRY, qualitative shape constraints can be imposed by the domain modeler for a concept <u>C</u>, by adding axioms like:

   <u>C</u> $\sqsubseteq$ GeometricPrimitive   // *primitives only*
   <u>C</u> $\sqsubseteq$ GPi   // *one particular GP only* ,

Quantitative parameters of a primitive can be modelled using so-called *concrete domain axioms*. An example is: **GPi** $\sqsubseteq$ $\exists$**hasWidth**, where **hasWidth** has range integer. Concrete domain axioms can also be used for expressing quantitative parameter ranges: **GP2** $\sqsubseteq$ $\exists$**hasWidth**.$_{\geq 200}$ $\sqcap$ $\exists$**hasWidth**.$_{<300}$. This contribution does not make use of concrete domains and the reader is referred to, for example, (Baader et al. 2003) for reference. As a general rule, it is recommended to only include information that is needed for logical inference, for the sake of simplicity of the ontology.

For providing semantics to the concept names, each **GPi** needs to be grounded (in logical terms) or mapped (in mathematical terms) to a subset of a quantitative geometry model space. Only when such a grounding is available, a qualitative ABox scene description can be mapped to a set of quantitative scene geometries. The grounding of the **GPi** concepts in quantitative geometry models must be done by the domain modeler in the ontology documentation.

4.2.2 Relative Object Pose

The relative pose between individuals is typically modelled using so-called *spatial calculi*. A spatial calculus is a qualitative abstraction of a quantitative parameter space (e. g. relative angular position $\in [0, 360)$) by a finite set of relations (e. g. **northOf, southOf, eastOf, westOf**). A multitude of spatial calculi have been proposed in the literature, addressing different kinds of spatial information (e. g. distance, orientation, topology, size) and different geometric entities (e. g. points, line segments). For an overview, see (Cohn and Renz 2007) or (Wallgrün et al. 2006). Spatial calculi have however only been axiomatised in First Order Logic, intuitionistic logic, and modal logic, but not yet in Description Logic, due to decidability reasons (Wessel 2001).

Formalisation of Base Relations

Subsequently, spatial calculi are formalised for the decidable DL $\mathcal{SHIQ}$, which necessarily comes at the cost of incomplete inference with respect to their intended semantics. Therefore, an approximating design pattern will be provided, which uses the named role closures introduced in Sec. 4.1.1. The formalisation is exemplified for the well-known *Region Connection Calculus (RCC)*.

The RCC8 calculus describes the degree of overlap between two regions using eight base relations. Figure 4.1 displays the semantics for each relation. For a formal introduction the reader is referred to (Randell et al. 1992). The implementation of the calculus in $\mathcal{SHIQ}$ comprises the following role inclusion axioms:

$\mathcal{T}_{RCC8} = \{$
  // Any calculus is a subrole of spatialRelation
  rcc8 $\sqsubseteq$ spatialRelation ,
  // Declaration of calculus role names
  dc $\sqsubseteq$ rcc8 ,
  ec $\sqsubseteq$ rcc8 ,

4.2. MODELLING OF SCENE GEOMETRY

$$\begin{aligned}
&\text{po} &&\sqsubseteq \text{rcc8} &&,\\
&\text{tpp} &&\sqsubseteq \text{rcc8} &&,\\
&\text{tppi} &&\sqsubseteq \text{rcc8} &&,\\
&\text{ntpp} &&\sqsubseteq \text{rcc8} &&,\\
&\text{ntppi} &&\sqsubseteq \text{rcc8} &&,\\
&\text{eq} &&\sqsubseteq \text{rcc8} &&,
\end{aligned}$$

// Declaration of role inverses

$$\begin{aligned}
&\text{tppi} &&\equiv \text{tpp}^- &&,\\
&\text{ntppi} &&\equiv \text{ntpp}^-
\end{aligned}$$

} .

With the exception of tpp and ntpp and their inverses, all roles are declared symmetric. The role eq is declared reflexive. If reflexive roles cannot be declared in a DL dialect, it can be approximated with the simple rule: $(x_2, x_1) : \text{eq} \Leftarrow (x_1, x_2) : \text{eq}$. A slightly coarser calculus is yielded by replacing tpp and ntpp and their inverses by pp ("proper part") and its inverse ppi. This coarser calculus will be referred to as rcc6 and be used in the remainder of this contribution.

Formalisation of Composition Tables

Spatial reasoning relies on algebraic operators on the relations, as introduced in Section 3.2.1, the most important of which is the composition operator. If the compositions of the base relations are computable, they can be stored in a *composition table* and reasoning about compositions becomes a matter of table look-ups. The composition table states for each pair of base relations r and s, which base relations r_i can possibly result from their concatenation:

$$r \circ s \sqsubseteq r_1 \sqcup \ldots \sqcup r_n \ .$$

Examples for such entries are

$$\begin{aligned}
&\text{pp} \circ \text{pp} \sqsubseteq \text{pp} && \textit{// pp is transitive}\\
&\text{eq} \circ r_i \sqsubseteq r_i && \textit{// eq is reflexive}
\end{aligned} \quad .$$

As $\mathcal{SHIQ}$ does not provide for role constructors, the entries of the composition table cannot be axiomatised in this language[4]. By using trigger rules (cf. Sec. 3.4)

---

[4] At least transitivity could be declared for roles in $\mathcal{SHIQ}$. However, qualitative number restrictions are no longer permitted for such roles (cf. Sec. 3.2.1). Since this type of restriction plays an essential role in the Computer Vision domain, declaration of transitivity should be omitted in this language.

4. DL FORMALISATION OF SCENE UNDERSTANDING

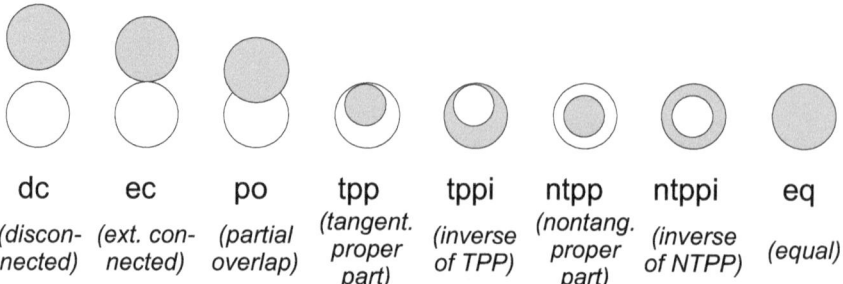

Figure 4.1: RCC8 calculus. Names and semantics of base relations.

instead, at least those entries not involving disjunctions[5] can be formalised on an ABox level:

$$(x_1, x_3) : \mathsf{pp} \Leftarrow (x_1, x_2) : \mathsf{pp} \land (x_2, x_3) : \mathsf{pp}$$
$$(x_1, x_3) : \mathsf{po} \Leftarrow (x_1, x_2) : \mathsf{eq} \land (x_2, x_3) : \mathsf{po}$$
$$\ldots$$

The axiomatisation of composition tables makes sense if not all spatial relations between individuals are provided in the ABox by the user. In this case it makes explicit the implicitly holding relations. They are also required if spatial relations need to be checked for consistency. They are not required if the ABox is known to be correct and complete with respect to the calculus.

Formalisation of JEPD semantics

The base relations of spatial calculi have a *jointly exhaustive and pairwise disjoint (JEPD)* semantics. This means that, for the case of RCC, each pair of **SceneObject** individuals is related via exactly one RCC base relation. An axiomatisation of JEPD would require role axioms of the form:

    // Role covering axiom
    rcc6 ≡ dc ⊔ ec ⊔ po ⊔ pp ⊔ ppi ⊔ eq

---

[5] In principle, disjunction in the rule consequence can be realised by using the joint superrole of all disjuncts in the rule consequence. However, as role coverage and role disjointness are not expressible in $\mathcal{SHIQ}$, no further inferences could be drawn from such a rule.

4.2. MODELLING OF SCENE GEOMETRY

// Role disjointness axioms
dc ⊑ ¬ec ⊓ ¬po ⊓ ¬pp ⊓ ¬ppi ⊓ ¬eq
ec ⊑ ...
...

Unfortunately, $\mathcal{SHIQ}$ does not support role constructors. While the ⊓ - and ⊔ - constructors could nevertheless be expressed by using role inclusion axioms, neither ≡ (role covering) nor ¬ (role complement) are expressible. Rules cannot be used for their approximation, as the required negation is not permitted in the rule consequence.

Example 4.5. The lacking expressiveness for role disjointness leads to incomplete reasoning with respect to the intended calculus semantics under some circumstances. Given the TBox $\mathcal{T}_{RCC6}$ as defined above and the ABox $\mathcal{A} = \{(road_{02}, lane_{01}) : \text{dc}\}$, the reasoner will not be able to infer that the two individuals must not be additionally, e. g., pp-related. This will lead to counterintuitive behaviour of the reasoner, for example when using named closed concepts (cf. Sec. 4.1.1) and role complements in a definition:

$\mathcal{KB} = \mathcal{T}_{RCC6} \cup \{$
  OneWayRoadNorth ≡ Road ⊓ ¬∃pp.OneWayLaneSouth ,
  OneWayLaneSouth ⊑ ClosedWorldConcept ,
  $road_{02}$: Road ,
  $lane_{01}$: OneWayLaneSouth ,
  $(road_{02}, lane_{01})$: dc
$\}$

According to this KB, $road_{02}$ does not possess a OneWayLaneSouth, as the only existing lane of that type is disconnected (dc) to it. Therefore one would expect the reasoner to infer that it is a OneWayRoadNorth: $\mathcal{KB} \models road_{02}$: OneWayRoadNorth. However, it cannot be deduced that the lane must not additionally be a proper part (pp) of that road: $\mathcal{KB} \not\models (road_{02}, lane_{01}) : \neg\text{pp}$. Therefore this relevant conclusion cannot be drawn. ∎

An axiomatisation of role disjointness is therefore clearly required. An approximation using the procedural extension of the KB will be sketched in the following.

Approximation to Role Disjointness

An ABox $\mathcal{A}$ will be denoted $\mathcal{R}$-*complete* with respect to a spatial calculus $\mathcal{R}$, if, for each pair of explicitly named SceneObject individuals (ind_i, ind_j), exactly one role assertion $(ind_i, ind_j) : r$ is contained in $\mathcal{A}$, with r being one of $\mathcal{R}$'s base relations. For m named individuals, this results in m^2 role assertions per calculus in $\mathcal{A}$. In such an ABox, the spatial arrangement of all named individuals is uniquely specified with respect to $\mathcal{R}$. On the Computer Vision side, this amounts to assuming that the relative spatial relations of the *detected* scene objects (*not* of all objects) can be computed by image processing, which is straightforward if the object geometry is approximately known (for many calculi a bounding box is enough). If the inverse of each non-symmetric and non-reflexive base relation is provided in the TBox (as was done for RCC6 here), the number of required explicit assertions can be slightly reduced without loosing completeness. One explicit assertion per pair of different individual names, permutations excluded, then suffices, resulting in a total of $\binom{m}{2}$ assertions.

For approximating role disjointness as sketched below, an $\mathcal{R}$-complete ABox is required with respect to ClosedWorldConcept individuals: Each ClosedWorldConcept individual must be contained in exactly one $\mathcal{R}$ role assertion for each named SceneObject individual. The following rule design pattern tests for $\mathcal{R}$-completeness of an ABox:

Pattern ABOX_CHECK:

Effect: Tests the ClosedWorldIndividuals of an ABox for completeness with respect to a spatial calculus. Yields inconsistent ABox if incomplete.

Parameter: r̲ calculus name (e.g. rcc6)

Template:

$x_2 : \bot \Leftarrow x_1 :$ ClosedWorldConcept $\land$ neg$((x_1, x_2) :$ r̲$)$

The ABox from Example 4.5 is $\mathcal{T}_{RCC6}$-complete[6], as with one ClosedWorldConcept individual ($lane_{01}$) and one other SceneObject individual ($road_{02}$), it requires only one RCC6 role assertion.

For an ABox which is complete with respect to closed world individuals and all spatial calculi, the semantics of role disjointness can be approximated by simply closing all spatial relations:

---

[6]The inclusion axioms OneWayLaneSouth $\sqsubseteq$ SceneObject and Road $\sqsubseteq$ SceneObject were omitted there for brevity.

4.2. MODELLING OF SCENE GEOMETRY

Pattern SPATIAL_CLOSURE:

Effect: Approximate disjointness semantics for spatial relations, by asserting partial closure for all spatial base relations.
Parameters: $r_1, \ldots, r_n$ Complete set of implemented spatial calculi
Requires: Pattern LOCALLY_CLOSED_WORLD
Template:

$\mathcal{T}_{SPATIAL\_CLOSURE} = \{$
  spatialRelation $\sqsubseteq$ closedWorldRole ,
  r_1 $\sqsubseteq$ spatialRelation ,
  $\ldots$,
  r_n $\sqsubseteq$ spatialRelation $\}$

Using this simple template, Pattern LOCALLY_CLOSED_WORLD (Sec. 4.1.1) closes all spatial relations with respect to ClosedWorldIndividuals. This is done automatically with the procedural extension provided for this pattern. The partial closure leads to an approximation to disjointness semantics for all spatial base relations as is illustrated in the following example.

Example 4.6. Let $\mathcal{KB}$ now denote the KB from Example 4.5 enhanced by $\mathcal{T}_{RCC6} \cup \mathcal{T}_{SPATIAL\_CLOSURE}$, the latter instantiated for rcc6. Its procedural extension contains the following additional assertions:

$road_{02} : \exists_{\leq 1} dc.ClosedWorldConcept$
$road_{02} : \exists_{\leq 0} ec.ClosedWorldConcept$
$road_{02} : \exists_{\leq 0} po.ClosedWorldConcept$
$road_{02} : \exists_{\leq 0} pp.ClosedWorldConcept$
$road_{02} : \exists_{\leq 0} ppi.ClosedWorldConcept$
$road_{02} : \exists_{\leq 0} eq.ClosedWorldConcept$.

This now leads to the desired result: $\mathcal{KB} \models road_{02} :$ OneWayRoadNorth, as now $\mathcal{KB} \models (road_{02}, lane_{01}) : \neg pp$. ∎

4.2.3 Relational Scene Geometry

Modelling relational scene geometry can be viewed as imposing spatial restrictions on the hypothesis space of admissible relations between scene objects. An ABox violating any imposed restriction must be classified inconsistent by the reasoner.

Subsequently, it will be shown how a scene geometry model for a particular class of scenes (such as intersections) can be set up. First, several types of spatial restrictions are introduced. It is then shown how these restrictions can be specified in a graphical notation. Finally, this notation is translated into a set of TBox axioms. This set of axioms is named $\mathcal{T}_{SCENE\_GEOMETRY}$. It requires the model of object geometries, $\mathcal{T}_{OBJECT\_GEOMETRY}$ (Section 4.2.1), and the spatial calculi used, for example $\mathcal{T}_{RCC6}$ (Section 4.2.2).

The set of ABoxes that are consistent with respect to $\mathcal{T}_{SCENE\_GEOMETRY}$, that is the set of its logical models, forms the *hypothesis space*[7] of qualitative scene geometries. As a consequence of the OWA, if $\mathcal{T}_{SCENE\_GEOMETRY} = \{\}$, arbitrary spatialRelations may hold between any pair of GeometricPrimitive individuals. The more axioms are added, the smaller gets the size of the hypothesis space.

Types of Restrictions

The proposed geometry model makes use of three types of spatial restrictions. Given some spatial relation r, these are:

Domain restrictions: Restrict the set of concepts, whose instances are allowed to have an r-relation, to the subset $\{C_{r_{dom},1}, \ldots, C_{r_{dom},n}\}$.

Filler restrictions: For each concept $C_{r_{dom},i}$ in the domain of r, restrict the set of allowed fillers to the subset $\{C_{r_{fill},i,1}, \ldots, C_{r_{fill},i,m}\}$. The tuples $(C_{r_{dom},i}, C_{r_{fill},i,j})$ are called r-domain/range pairs.

Cardinality restrictions: For each r-domain/range pair $(C_{r_{dom},i}, C_{r_{fill},i,j})$, restrict the number of allowed fillers to the interval $[min_{r,i,j}, max_{r,i,j}]$.

A geometry model for a given class of scenes (such as intersections) is specified by providing each of these restrictions for each spatialRelation subrole.

The modelling level of detail for the domains and ranges may vary: They can be specified on a purely geometric level using the GPi concepts, or on the semantic level using concepts such as Road or Lane, or by a combination of both.

Graphical Specification of Geometry Model

Specifying a qualitative geometry model graphically facilitates understanding and integration with other Scene Understanding KB's. In the following, a

---

[7]Note that the elements of this hypothesis space are not disjoint: Hypotheses may be subsumed by other, more general ones, contrasting (Schröder 1999)'s requirement of maximally specific and thus disjoint models.

4.2. MODELLING OF SCENE GEOMETRY 63

graphical notation will be provided through which the restrictions introduced above can be specified graphically. Its translation into DL axioms to form $\mathcal{T}_{SCENE\_GEOMETRY}$ will be given afterwards.

To the best of the author's knowledge no standardised graphical notation language exists yet for DL[8]. Fig. 4.2 proposes a graphical notation based on the Unified Modelling Languages (UML), a widespread and standardised visual specification language in object-oriented programming.

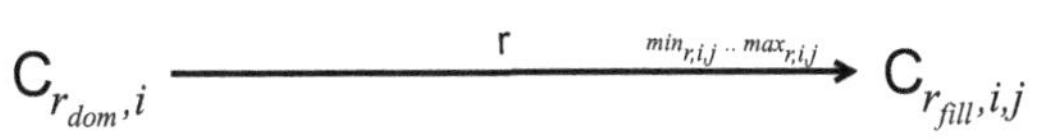

$$C_{r_{dom},i} \xrightarrow{r \quad min_{r,i,j} \cdots max_{r,i,j}} C_{r_{fill},i,j}$$

Figure 4.2: **Proposed graphical notation for specifying a qualitative scene geometry model.** Arrows represent roles and relate concepts. An r-labelled arrow is present between two concepts iff the two concepts form an r-domain/range pair as specified above. The corresponding cardinality constraint is then written beneath the arrow head. An omitted cardinality constraint is read as 0..∗. For symmetric and inverse roles the arrow has a head at both ends. An example of its use is given in Figure 4.3.

A geometry model is specified completely in this notation, if the set of depicted concepts covers the SceneObject concept, and if all allowed spatialRelation-domain/range pairs are specified by arrows according to Figure 4.2.

Transitivity and/or symmetry of a role must be made explicit in the graphical specification. For example, if r is transitive, and the model requires exactly one r-domain/range pair (C_1, C_2), and exactly one r-domain/range pair (C_2, C_3), this implies the presence of at least one r-domain/range pair (C_1, C_3). Thus the graphical model requires an arrow with a minimum cardinality equal to one between C_1 and C_2, between C_2 and C_3, *and* between C_1 and C_3.

Translation of Specification into DL

For any spatial relation r, the graphical specification is unambiguously translated into DL, with the semantics of the restrictions as defined above, as follows:

---

[8](Calvanese et al. 1998) proposes a representation based on Entity-Relationship models.

64　　　　　　　　　　4. DL FORMALISATION OF SCENE UNDERSTANDING

Pattern SCENE_GEOMETRY:

Effect: Translate geometry model for a given role $\underline{r}$ from the graphical notation specified in Fig. 4.2 to a set of DL axioms.

Parameters:
- $\underline{r}$ Atomic role
- $\underline{C_{r_{dom},1}}, \ldots, \underline{C_{r_{dom},n}}$ Set of allowed domains for $\underline{r}$
- $\underline{C_{r_{fill},1,1}}, \ldots, \underline{C_{r_{fill},n,m}}$ Set of allowed fillers for $\underline{r}$
- $\underline{min/max_{r,1,1}}, \ldots,$ Min/Max no restriction for
- $\underline{min/max_{r,n,m}}$ each $\underline{r}$-domain/range pair

Template:

$\mathcal{T}_{SCENE\_GEOMETRY} = \{$

// Domain constraint

$\neg(\underline{C_{r_{dom},1}} \sqcup \ldots \sqcup \underline{C_{r_{dom},n}}) \sqsubseteq \forall \underline{r}. \bot$,

// Tailored range constraints

$\underline{C_{r_{dom},1}} \sqsubseteq \forall \underline{r}.(\underline{C_{r_{fill},1,1}} \sqcup \ldots \sqcup \underline{C_{r_{fill},1,m}})$,

$\ldots$

$\underline{C_{r_{dom},n}} \sqsubseteq \forall \underline{r}.(\underline{C_{r_{fill},n,1}} \sqcup \ldots \sqcup \underline{C_{r_{fill},n,m}})$,

// Cardinality constraints

$\underline{C_{r_{dom},1}} \sqsubseteq \exists_{\geq \underline{min_{r,1,1}}} \underline{r}. \underline{C_{r_{fill},1,1}} \sqcap$
$\exists_{\leq \underline{max_{r,1,1}}} \underline{r}. \underline{C_{r_{fill},1,1}}$,

$\ldots$

$\underline{C_{r_{dom},1}} \sqsubseteq \exists_{\geq \underline{min_{r,1,m}}} \underline{r}. \underline{C_{r_{fill},1,m}} \sqcap$
$\exists_{\leq \underline{max_{r,1,m}}} \underline{r}. \underline{C_{r_{fill},1,m}}$,

$\ldots$

$\underline{C_{r_{dom},n}} \sqsubseteq \exists_{\geq \underline{min_{r,n,1}}} \underline{r}. \underline{C_{r_{fill},n,1}} \sqcap$
$\exists_{\leq \underline{max_{r,n,1}}} \underline{r}. \underline{C_{r_{fill},n,1}}$,

$\ldots$

$\underline{C_{r_{dom},n}} \sqsubseteq \exists_{\geq \underline{min_{r,n,m}}} \underline{r}. \underline{C_{r_{fill},n,m}} \sqcap$
$\exists_{\leq \underline{max_{r,n,m}}} \underline{r}. \underline{C_{r_{fill},n,m}}$,

$\}$

This template must be instantiated for all descendants of the **spatialRelation** role.

Example 4.7. Fig. 4.3 depicts a geometry model from the traffic domain using only the RCC6-calculus. It models a **Road** as having at least 1 **Lane** and 2

4.2. MODELLING OF SCENE GEOMETRY

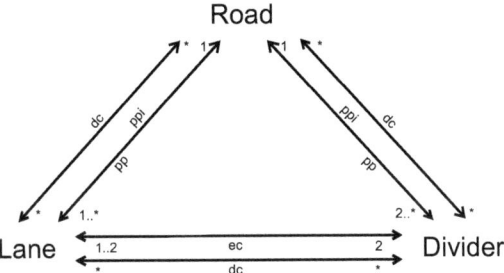

Figure 4.3: Example of a graphical specification of a geometry model for the traffic domain using the RCC6 calculus only.

Dividers as proper parts (pp), and Lanes and Dividers as being externally connected (ec) with the given cardinalities. The Lanes and Dividers are furthermore part of (ppi) exactly one Road. The model also states that besides "disconnected" (dc) no further relations must hold. For better readability, a role which may hold between arbitrary individuals, like dc here, can be left out from the graphical specification.

With respect to the pp-role, Pattern SCENE_GEOMETRY translates the graphical specification into DL as follows:

$\mathcal{T}_{SCENE\_GEOMETRY} \sqsubseteq \{$

// Domain constraint
¬Road $\sqsubseteq \forall pp. \bot$,

// Tailored range constraints
Road $\sqsubseteq \forall pp.$ (Lane $\sqcup$ Divider),

// Cardinality constraint
Road $\sqsubseteq \exists_{\geq 1} pp.$ Lane ,
Road $\sqsubseteq \exists_{\geq 2} pp.$ Divider
$\}$.

The remaining five rcc6 roles translate analogously. ∎

A particular drawback of modelling geometry with a DL language such as $\mathcal{SHIQ}$ is that role chains and role-value-maps are not supported, and therefore relations between three or more individuals cannot be constrained (cf. Sec. 3.4). For the given example, it is, e. g., not axiomatisable that a Divider and a Lane that are externally connected (ec) must be a proper part of (ppi) the *same* Road. A partial remedy for this lacking expressiveness, that is used in this contribution, is to close concepts and roles (cf. Sec.4.2.2): If the correct and complete set of dividers in ec-relation to a given lane is provided, along with the correct and complete set of ppi-relations with respect to the containing Road, and if completeness of the set of ec- and ppi-fillers is asserted, this implies that no further divider must be in ec-relation with that lane. This explicitly excludes all dividers from other roads.

4.3 Formalisation of Scene Understanding Tasks

4.3.1 Object Detection: KB Realization

Object detection refers to the discovery of a new scene object through object features detected by a sensor and/or through logical inference.

Example 4.8. As a simple example for object detection through inference, consider the axiom

$$\text{ArrowMarking} \sqsubseteq \exists \text{isPartOf.Lane} \ .$$

It implies the existence of a lane whenever an arrow marking is detected. Speaking in Computer Vision terms, an arrow is a sufficient *feature* or *vision cue* of lane objects. ∎

On the DL side, a detected object requires the automatic creation of a new individual. Although increasing the number of individuals is possible due to the open domain paradigm (cf. Sec. 4.1.1), the creation of new individuals is not covered by classical DL inference services. The usage of non-classical inference services is outside the scope of this contribution, but promising formalisms for follow-up work are discussed in the outlook section.

An alternative option, which is readily available with existing DL technology, is to preintroduce all hypothetically possible individuals. Given that a maximum of n individuals of class are potentially detectable in the scene, the corresponding design pattern reads as:

4.3. FORMALISATION OF SCENE UNDERSTANDING TASKS

Pattern OBJECT_DETECTION:

Effect: Introduce n object hypothesis that are to be verified (i.e. detected) or falsified, and constrain their potential types. Other parts of the KB can now classify them into verified or falsified.

Parameters:
- $\underline{n}$ — Maximum number of objects to be detected
- $\underline{C}_1, \ldots, \underline{C}_k$ — Types of objects to be detected (e.g. Car)

Template:

$\mathcal{T}_{OBJECT\_DETECTION} = \{$
 ObjectHypothesis $\equiv$ Verified $\sqcup$ Falsified ,
 disjoint(Verified, Falsified) ,
 ObjectHypothesis $\sqsubseteq$ ClosedWorldConcept ,
 Verified $\equiv \underline{C}_1 \sqcup \ldots \sqcup \underline{C}_k$ $\}$

$\mathcal{A}_{OBJECT\_DETECTION} = \{$
 $ind_{\underline{C}_1}$: ObjectHypothesis ,
 $\ldots$,
 $ind_{\underline{C}_n}$: ObjectHypothesis $\}$.

The first two axioms introduce an object hypothesis as a concept which can either be verified or falsified, but not both. A falsified hypothesis means that the object is provably *not* present in the scene. The third axiom builds on the introduced closures from Section 4.1.1 and axiomatises the "promise" that all hypothetical individuals will be explicitly introduced. The fourth axiom states which object types $\underline{C}_i$ are to be verified or falsified by the reasoner. An individual that is assigned an objec type $\underline{C}_i$ is automatically verified. In the ABox, n new individuals $ind_{\underline{C}_1}, \ldots, ind_{\underline{C}_n}$ are introduced as instances of ObjectHypothesis.

With this pattern, the task of object detection reduces to one of object classification (cf. next Subsection): Each individual $ind_{\underline{C}_i}$ can be classified as either $\underline{C}$, thereby implying Verified, or as Falsified in the course of reasoning. Individuals will remain unclassified if no sufficient classification information is available.

To prevent the number of individuals from blowing up, this pattern should be applied with care.

4.3.2 Object Classification: KB Realization

In Scene Interpretation, object classification refers to the task of assigning to a detected object one of n discrete labels, so called classes. Speaking in DL terms, an individual *ind* of class C is to be specialised into one of C's subclasses. The corresponding pattern reads as:

Pattern OBJECT_CLASSIFICATION:

Effect: Introduce a discrete set of subclasses ("labels") for a class C ("classification task"). Assign individuals to be classified to class C. Other parts of the KB can now specialise ("classify") into subclasses.

Parameters:
C — Super class to be specialised (e.g. Vehicle)
$Label_1 \sqcup \ldots \sqcup Label_n$ — Class labels (e.g. Car, Motorcycle,...)
$\underline{ind_1}, \ldots, \underline{ind_m}$ — Names of individuals to be classified with respect to C

Template:

$\mathcal{T}_{OBJECT\_CLASSIFICATION} = \{$
  C $\equiv$ $Label_1 \sqcup \ldots \sqcup Label_n$ // coverage of superclass ,
  // or
  C $\sqsupseteq$ $Label_1 \sqcup \ldots \sqcup Label_n$ // no coverage of superclass ,
  disjoint($Label_1, \ldots, Label_n$)   // optional $\}$.

$\mathcal{A}_{OBJECT\_CLASSIFICATION} = \{$
  $\underline{ind_1}$: C ,
  $\ldots$;
  $\underline{ind_m}$: C $\}$.

If individuals shall be allowed to not belong to any of the $Label_i$ subclasses, the second axiom must be chosen, otherwise the first. The disjointness axiom must be added if membership to more than one subclass shall be disallowed. Each $Label_i$ class can in turn be specialised into a set of subclasses, to define a further, more specialised classification task. This way, hierarchies of classes are built, so called *taxonomies* (see also Section 3.3.1).

Using this pattern, the standard inference task of *ABox realization* as described in Section 3.3.2.3 automatically classifies any individual of class C. In contrast to common non-logic classifiers, as standard DL inference services perform deductive reasoning, an individual is classified only if membership to a subclass can be proven (even if the equality axiom in the template is used).

A particular strength of logic-based classification is its support for *multiple inher-*

4.3. FORMALISATION OF SCENE UNDERSTANDING TASKS

itance, a term borrowed from object-oriented programming which denotes that an individual is allowed to be an instance of several superclasses: $ind : C_1 \sqcap \ldots \sqcap C_k$. ABox realization therefore solves $k \cdot m$ classification tasks at once, k being the number of single classification tasks and m being the number of individuals. Because of the mutual dependencies between the single classification tasks in relational domains such as Scene Interpretation (e.g. car detection strongly influences lane detection, and vice versa), a joint classifier can tremendously reduce the hypothesis space of each such task, an essential quality in the high-dimensional spaces typical for Scene Interpretation (cf. Chapter 1). This is called *collective classification* in the relational classification literature (Taskar et al. 2002).

4.3.3 Link Prediction: Entailment

Link prediction refers to the task of predicting (a) the existence and (b) the types of relationships between individuals in a relational domain (e. g. (Taskar et al. 2004)). Link prediction has mainly been studied in the context of social network analysis and mining of web pages. However, together with collective classification, it is likely to have great impact within the next decade's Computer Vision research, representing the transition from single object recognition to relational Scene Interpretation.

Speaking in DL terms, the types of relationships correspond to the respective child roles of a given role, and thus (b) equals the specialisation of a holding relation r between two individuals into some child role. In principle, an analogy to Pattern OBJECT_CLASSIFICATION adapted to roles could be applied:

$$\mathcal{T} = \{$$
$$\underline{r} \equiv \underline{childR_1} \sqcup \ldots \sqcup \underline{childR_n}$$
// or
$$\underline{r} \sqsupseteq \underline{childR_1} \sqcup \ldots \sqcup \underline{childR_n},$$
$$\text{disjoint}(\underline{childR_1}, \ldots, \underline{childR_n}) \text{ // optional}$$
$$\}.$$

Collective role classification could then be performed via ABox *entailment* (cf. Sec. 3.3.2.3), i. e. asking whether $\mathcal{KB} \models (ind_i, ind_j) : \underline{childR_k}$ for all individual pairs (ind_i, ind_j). The corresponding tailored RACERPRO command reads as: (related-individuals childRk). However, as $\mathcal{SHIQ}$ neither knows role disjointness nor role covering axioms, this template is not axiomatisable. An alternative – and less elegant – way of coding is via trigger rules. Care has to be taken here, too, as the law of contraposition does not hold for trigger rules. In summary, link prediction exploiting all available information is not axiomatisable in this DL dialect.

4.3.4 Data Association: Unification

The term *data association* has been coined in the context of data fusion in a multisensor and multitarget detection and tracking scenario. Originally, it denotes the assignment of new sensor measurements to already existing objects or object tracks (Bar-Shalom 1987). In a broader sense, it also denotes the identification of a set of object measurements as referring to one and the same scene object.

In formal logic, data association requires the ability of inferring semantic equality between two differently named individuals: $\mathcal{KB} \models ind_i = ind_j$. This reasoning service is known as *entity resolution*, *unification reasoning*, or simply *identification*, and is a classic DL reasoning task. Obviously, unification requires the unique name assumption to be abandoned.

An implementation of unification reasoning can build on the *distributed sensors* scenario introduced in Section 4.1.2. It merely requires the procedural KB extension as described in Algorithm 2, which provides for local disjointness axioms and for named role closure. The provided Example 4.3 already exemplifies unification reasoning. In RACERPRO, unification reasoning is performed using the query:

```
(individual-synonyms indi)    .
```

All those individuals will be returned for which semantic equality with ind_i can be unambiguously inferred, and remain unidentified otherwise. Just as for object classification, this poses a key difference to non-DL association techniques, which usually prefer uncertain association over no association.

4.4 Summary

This section has elaborated on the feasibility of mapping important Scene Interpretation characteristics into the DL dialect $\mathcal{SHIQ}$. For the cases in which no straightforward correspondence existed, KB engineering guidelines in the form of DL design patterns have been provided.

It has been shown that an unknown number of objects corresponds to DL's open domain assumption, and that partiality of sensor data corresponds to DL's open world assumption. Local completeness of data, on the other hand, has been shown

4.4. SUMMARY

to be not axiomatisable. An approximation has been provided on the assertional level. It has furthermore been argued that a redundant multi-sensor setting can be realised when abandoning the unique name assumption, which can be switched on and off in modern DL implementations. A design pattern has been provided, which formally characterises the properties of four different classes of sensors, namely complementary vs. redundant sensors delivering data on a feature- vs. object-level.

A hypothesis space of qualitative scene geometries has been proposed. It is composed of two main components: A discrete set of admissible geometries for each object, and a discrete set of admissible spatial relations between each pair of objects. Modelling scene geometry can be viewed as imposing restrictions on the admissible object geometries and on the admissible spatial relations. For modelling a hypothesis space for a particular class of scenes, a visual notation has been proposed, along with its translation to a DL axiom set.

The axiomatisation of spatial calculi has turned out unsatisfactory, as it requires role constructors –namely role disjointness and role covering– which are not available in this DL dialect. However, if the spatial relations between detected objects are given by the Computer Vision system, role disjointness can be approximated. A corresponding design pattern has been provided.

Four crucial Scene Interpretation tasks have been examined with respect to their solvability by classic DL reasoning. These were namely object detection, object classification, link prediction, and data association. When confined to classical DL inference, object detection can only be tackled by preintroducing the maximum possible number of individuals present in the scene. A corresponding design pattern has been provided. Collective object classification is readily available in DL via the reasoning service of ABox realization. The association of data acquired by multiple, redundant sensors is also readily solvable in DL through identification reasoning. The task of link prediction, by contrast, cannot be performed in dialects without role constructors.

The ultimate reasoning service for Scene Interpretation would be the automatic construction of the set of all scene hypotheses, that is the set of all possible logical models of the KB. To perform this task, the realm of monotonic, deductive reasoning would have to be abandoned. A discussion about promising non-monotonic KR formalisms can be found in the outlook of this thesis.

The DL knowledge engineering approaches described in this chapter form the basis of the Scene Interpretation system for Intersection Understanding, which will be presented in the following two chapters.

5 RONNY: The Road Network Ontology

This chapter introduces the **Ro**ad **N**etwork **On**tology (RONNY). It is a DL TBox implemented in the dialect $\mathcal{SHIQ}$, modelling the qualitative geometry and building regulations of roads and their intersections for the purpose of Scene Understanding. Section 5.1 introduces the RONNY vocabulary, that is the set of its concept and relation names. This vocabulary is used for setting up a geometry model in Section 5.2, and for modelling a set of road building regulations for roads and their intersections in Section 5.3. The KB modelling techniques introduced in Chapter 4 will be extensively applied throughout this chapter.

The modelling goal is a hypothesis space of intersection geometries and semantics that has a large expressiveness (a wide variety of complex intersections can be represented), while at the same time it maintains a feasible size (through imposing restrictive high-level constraints).

Creating a RONNY ABox from sensor data, and applying DL reasoning to solve several Scene Understanding tasks, will be described and evaluated in Chapter 6.

5.1 Symbol Grounding

The most elementary concepts and roles present in a DLKB are called *primitives*. Their counterparts are *defineables*, which are defined (using the $\equiv$-constructor) out of other KB concepts and roles. The semantics of a primitive must be provided by documentation relating it to some real world entity, while the semantics of a defineable is given by its definition. Providing semantics to a symbolic representation is called *symbol grounding*.

The following Sections 5.1.1–5.1.4 axiomatise and ground RONNY's primitive concepts and relations. For easy readability, the axiomatisation is provided graphically in the form of *taxonomies*[1]. The primitives are grouped into the set of *scene object* concepts, the set of qualitative *object geometry* concepts, the set of *spatial relations*, and the set of *functional concepts* and *functional relations*. Finally,

---
[1] A mapping of a taxonomy into DL axioms is provided in Pattern OBJECT_CLASSIFICATION (Section 4.3.2).

Section 5.1.5 derives a set of defineables from these primitives, which will prove useful for compactly formalising the road building regulations later on.

5.1.1 Taxonomy of SceneObjects

The following figure depicts RONNY's taxonomy of SceneObject primitives[2]:

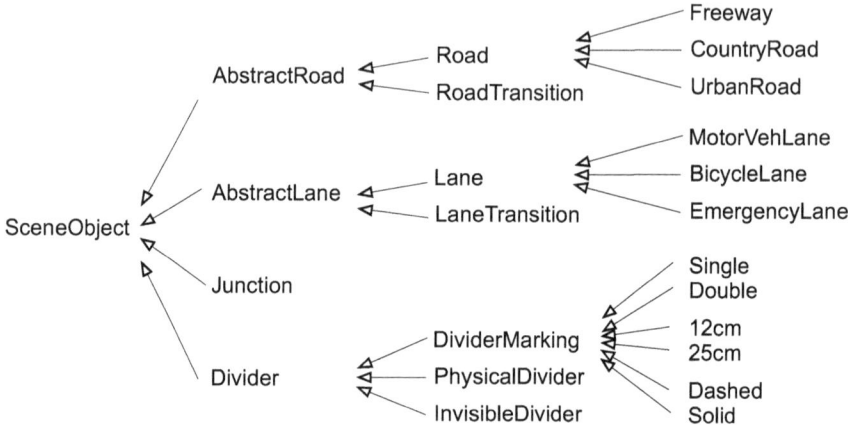

Figure 5.1: Taxonomy of SceneObject Concept Primitives. Up to the 3rd hierarchy layer, all concepts are mutually disjoint and jointly cover the superclass. Disjointness and covering information for 4th layer concepts is given in the text.

The primitives are grounded as follows:

SceneObject	A physically existent object that is potentially present in the considered scenes and that is relevant to the particular Scene Understanding task. The qualitative geometry of a SceneObject can be modeled/inferred (cf. Pattern OBJECT_GEOMETRY (Section 4.2.1)).
Abstract*	A term borrowed from object oriented programming: A concept with this prefix requires its individuals to be explicitly specialised into one of its children.
AbstractLane	A scene object on which driving in longitudinal direction is permitted according to road traffic regulations. It is laterally aligned with two Dividers.

---

[2]Concepts which are covered by their children are still referred to as primitives here, although formally they are exhaustively defined by their children.

5.1. SYMBOL GROUNDING

AbstractRoad	An aggregate for a set of laterally aligned and alternating Lanes and Dividers.
Road	An AbstractRoad which is *not* part of a Junction. It can be either a Freeway (German: "Autobahn"), a CountryRoad (German: "Landstraße"), or an UrbanRoad. These types are disjoint and jointly cover the Road class. It can be longitudinally aligned on one or both ends to RoadTransitions on a Junction.
Lane	An AbstractLane which is *not* part of a Junction. It can be designated for bicycles, motor vehicles, or be an emergency lane. The latter is disjoint from the former two, while the former two are not disjoint from each other (as many UrbanRoads permit cars and bicycles on a single lane). The three types cover the Lane class. Bus lanes have not yet been modelled.
*Transition	A set of *Transitions constitutes a Junction. *Transitions longitudinally connect pairs of Roads and pairs of Lanes. The existence of a *Transition between two Roads or two Lanes indicates that driving from one to the other is permitted according to road traffic regulations without performing a lane change, This is subsequently referred to as a *driveable path*. Note that, contrary to general usage of the term, a driveable path must not require a lane change.
RoadTransition	An AbstractRoad which is part of a Junction. It is longitudinally aligned with two Roads.
LaneTransition	An AbstractLane which is part of a Junction. It is longitudinally aligned with two Lanes.
Junction	An aggregate for a set of *Transitions, which may geometrically overlap. Allows traffic participants to transit between two Roads. Already a single RoadTransition between only two Roads qualifies as a Junction.
Divider	Visually separates two Lanes within one Road. It can either be of type marking, physical (like a road curb or a guardrail), or be omitted. Divider markings can be either a single or a double line, be either 12cm or 25cm wide, and be either dashed or solid. Each pair is disjoint and covers the DividerMarking class.

The informal expressions used for denoting spatial relations (like "laterally aligned") will be formally introduced and grounded in Section 5.1.3.

5.1.2 Taxonomy of GeometricPrimitives

According to Pattern OBJECT_GEOMETRY (Section 4.2.1), a qualitative object geometry model requires introducing a finite set of GeometricPrimitive concepts, and grounding them in quantitative geometry models.

RONNY introduces the three primitives GP1, GP2 and GP3 depicted in 5.2(a). Their symbol grounding is provided graphically by Figure 5.2(b). The following

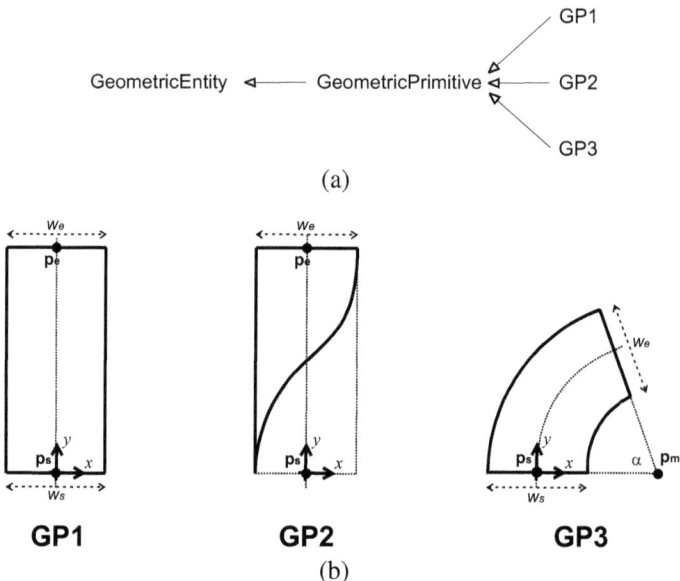

Figure 5.2: Geometric Primitives. Grounding of GeometricPrimitive concepts *(a)* in geometry models *(b)*. The $\mathbf{p}_s, \mathbf{p}_e, \mathbf{p}_m$ are 2-element vectors given in earth-fixed cartesian coordinates. Start and end widths $w_s[m], w_e[m]$ are positive scalars, the arc length α of GP3 is $\in [\frac{1}{4}\pi, \pi]$ and its radius $r = \|\mathbf{p}_s - \mathbf{p}_m\|$ is $\in [3m, 30m]$ (empirically chosen). The sketch of GP1 and GP2 is simplified in that their spine, i.e. the curve connecting $\mathbf{p}_s$ and $\mathbf{p}_e$, is a Hermite spline instead of a straight line segment. Therefore, they possess the additional parameters t_s and t_e (not depicted here), denoting the orientation of the tangents at $\mathbf{p}_s$ and $\mathbf{p}_e$, respectively.

remarks concerning coordinate systems are required in addition: RONNY assumes a *locally flat earth*, and all coordinates are given as two-dimensional projections onto this ground plane. Two types of coordinate systems are applied. The quanti-

5.1. SYMBOL GROUNDING

tative parameters of the GPi are given with respect to a *geocentric* (termed earth-fixed or absolute in engineering literature) cartesian system using UTM coordinates. UTM is a global cartesian system, its origin being the central meridian, using units of metres, that is widely used for georeferencing maps. The second type are *egocentric* (termed object-centred or local in engineering literature) cartesian systems inherent to each individual of class GeometricPrimitive. A grounding of a GPi must therefore include the position of its local coordinate system (cf. Fig. 5.2). Spatial relations among GeometricPrimitives are always given with respect to the egocentric system (note that this implies that a relation such as eastOf is not transitive). For simplicity, it is currently assumed that primitives, which are not part of a junction, are grounded such that their y-axis points toward the junction. For ABoxes containing only one junction, this allows to omit axioms dealing with qualitative coordinate transformation.

This thesis focuses on estimating qualitative intersection geometry (such as: "Is lane transition *lt* of geometric shape GP1, GP2 or GP3?"). Estimating the quantitative parameters of the GPi using Computer Vision techniques is beyond its scope. (Hummel et al. 2007), (Yang 2006), and (Pink and Hummel 2008) (the latter in the context of vehicle localisation) provide reasonable start estimates for these parameters using a similar geometry model. The parameters are set based on the given coordinates and tangents of p_s and p_e for those GPi of class Road that are provided by a commercial digital map, and a deterministic set of equations for derivation of the other parameters.

5.1.3 Taxonomy of spatialRelations

RONNY uses a set of spatial descriptors[3] to describe the relative position between GeometricPrimitives. Three basic descriptors are used, namely the *degree of overlap*, the *relative position* and the *relative orientation* between two individuals. The former is based on the RCC6 calculus (cf. Section 4.2.2), the latter two are formalised below. Based on these descriptors and role forming constructors, three composed descriptors describing spatial *alignedness*, *neighbourhood* and *relative heading*[4] of primitives will be defined afterwards.

---

[3]The term spatial descriptor is used in this chapter instead of the term spatial calculus that was introduced in Section 4.2.2. A spatial calculus requires the definition of a set of operations on its base relations (cf. e.g. (Wallgrün et al. 2006)), not all of which are provided for the relations used here.

[4]Initially both, basic descriptors and composed descriptors, had been implemented in RONNY, and the latter – due to lack of role forming constructors in $\mathcal{SHIQ}$ – were derived using trigger rules. This approach was abandoned due to reasons of computational complexity and incompleteness of inference (role disjointness and role coverage cannot be axiomatised this way (cf. Sec. 4.2.2)). Only the composed descriptors became actual part of the implementation. The basic descriptors are used in this

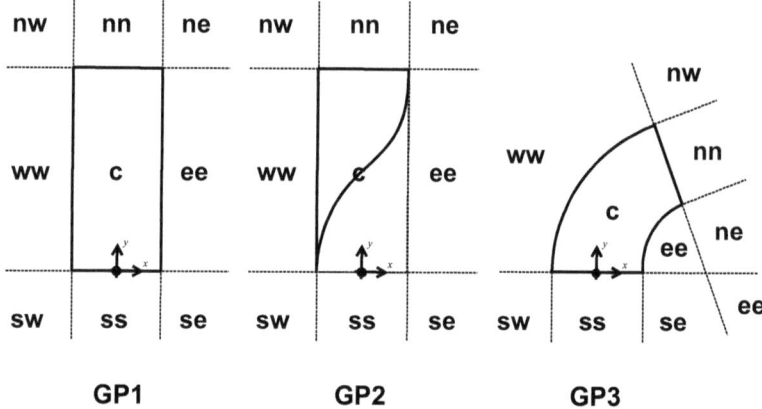

Figure 5.3: Relative Position. Definition of the cardinal direction "bins" as introduced by the relPosition-descriptor for the geometric primitives GP1-GP3.

Relative Position

The relative position between two individuals is modelled using relative cardinal directions:

$\mathcal{T}_{RelPosition} = \{$
relPosition	$\sqsubseteq$ spatialRelation	
nn	$\sqsubseteq$ relPosition	// "north of" ,
ne	$\sqsubseteq$ relPosition	// "northeast of" ,
...		
sw	$\sqsubseteq$ relPosition	// "southwest of" ,
ww	$\sqsubseteq$ relPosition	// "west of" ,
c	$\sqsubseteq$ relPosition	// "centred on" $\}$,

given relative to the element's egocentric coordinate system. Consequently, no base relation is symmetric, transitive or has an inverse. The reflexive role c ("centred on") is provided merely to ensure the descriptors' JEPD property (cf. Sec. 4.2.2).

In addition, a coarser set of four cardinal directions is defined from the above roles. Note that these roles are not disjoint any more:

$nn \sqcup ne \sqcup nw \sqsubseteq n$
$ss \sqcup se \sqcup sw \sqsubseteq s$
$ne \sqcup ee \sqcup se \sqsubseteq e$
$nw \sqcup ww \sqcup sw \sqsubseteq w$.

---

documentation for grounding the composed descriptors by formal definition.

5.1. Symbol Grounding

Each **GeometricPrimitive** needs to provide a definition for the cardinal direction "bins" in the Cartesian Plane. For GP1-GP3 these definitions are given geometrically by Figure 5.3. Given a pair of **GeometricPrimitives** (ind_{ref}, ind_{filler}), the relPosition-descendant is determined by the position of ind_{filler}'s centre of mass relative to ind_{ref}. For individuals composed of several GPi (i. e. those that are a **GeometricEntity** but not a **GeometricPrimitive** anymore), the relative pose is defined by evaluating the above measure for that pair of contained **GeometricPrimitives** with the closest distance.

Relative Orientation

The qualitative relative orientation between two individuals is modelled using the following symmetric base relations:

$$T_{RelOrientation} = \{$$
$$\text{relOrientation} \quad \sqsubseteq \text{spatialRelation}$$
$$\| \quad \sqsubseteq \text{relOrientation} \quad // \text{"parallel"},$$
$$L \quad \sqsubseteq \text{relOrientation} \quad // \text{"perpendicular"},$$
$$X \quad \sqsubseteq \text{relOrientation} \quad // \text{"oblique"}, \quad \} .$$

The base relations are grounded using a measure of orientation difference β between the primitives' spines. Each **GeometricPrimitive** needs to provide a definition of its spine. Those definitions are provided in Figure 5.4. Note that according to the text below Figure 5.2(b), the spines of GP1 and GP2 are, in fact, Hermite splines. A simple measure of orientation difference between two curves is the average orientation difference between their start tangents t_s and their end tangents t_e (cf. Fig. 5.2(b)). Special treatment is required, however, for comparing a GP3 with a GP1 or GP2. These primitives should be in a ||-relation when either their start or their end orientations are equal. In this case, the orientation similarity is given by the orientation difference between the two start tangents, iff the start points have closer Euclidean distance than the end points, and between the two end tangents otherwise. All base relations are consequently symmetric, but not transitive.

Given the orientation difference β the following grounding was used:

$$(ind_i, ind_j) : \begin{cases} \| & , \beta \in [0°, 15°) \vee (165°, 180°) \\ L & , \beta \in (75°, 105°) \\ X & , \text{otherwise} \end{cases} .$$

For individuals that are composed of several **GeometricPrimitives**, the orienta-

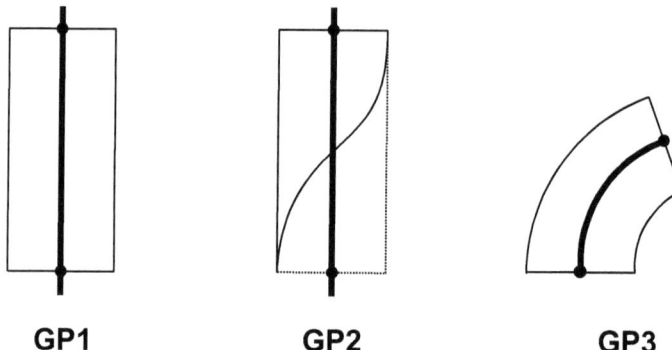

Figure 5.4: Relative Orientation. Definition of the spines of the geometric primitives GP1-GP3 as required by the relOrientation-descriptor.

tion difference is defined by evaluating the above measure for that pair of contained GeometricPrimitives with the closest distance.

Spatial Alignedness

The basic descriptors $\mathcal{T}_{RCC6}$, $\mathcal{T}_{RelPosition}$ and $\mathcal{T}_{RelOrientation}$ are used to ground several *composed descriptors* by formal definition. Since role forming constructors are not present in $\mathcal{SHIQ}$, these definitions are not part of the implementation. The composed descriptors describe several spatial arrangements of GeometricPrimitives that are particularly relevant to the intersection domain. The first descriptor is termed $\mathcal{T}_{Alignedness}$ and is defined as follows:

$\mathcal{T}_{Alignedness} = \{$
   alignedRelation $\sqsubseteq$ spatialRelation ,
   alignedRelation $\equiv$ northAlignedWith $\sqcup$ southAlignedWith $\sqcup$
                                   eastAlignedWith $\sqcup$ westAlignedWith $\sqcup$
                                     alignedWithPart $\sqcup$ alignedPartOf $\sqcup$
                                     notAligned ,
   northAlignedWith $\equiv$ alignedRelation $\sqcap$ nn $\sqcap$ ec $\sqcap$ ∥ ,
   southAlignedWith $\equiv$ alignedRelation $\sqcap$ ss $\sqcap$ ec $\sqcap$ ∥ ,
   eastAlignedWith $\equiv$ alignedRelation $\sqcap$ ee $\sqcap$ ec $\sqcap$ ∥ ,
   westAlignedWith $\equiv$ alignedRelation $\sqcap$ ww $\sqcap$ ec $\sqcap$ ∥ ,
   alignedWithPart $\equiv$ alignedRelation $\sqcap$ (eq $\sqcup$ pp) $\sqcap$ ∥ ,

5.1. Symbol Grounding

$\qquad$ alignedPartOf $\quad \equiv$ alignedWithPart$^-$,
$\qquad$ notAligned $\quad \equiv$ alignedRelation ⊓
$\qquad\qquad\qquad\qquad$ ¬northAlignedWith ⊓
$\qquad\qquad\qquad\qquad$ ¬southAlignedWith ⊓
$\qquad\qquad\qquad\qquad$ ¬westAlignedWith ⊓
$\qquad\qquad\qquad\qquad$ ¬eastAlignedWith ⊓
$\qquad\qquad\qquad\qquad$ ¬alignedWithPart ⊓
$\qquad\qquad\qquad\qquad$ ¬alignedPartOf $\qquad\qquad$ } .

Only notAligned is symmetric, and alignedWithPart is reflexive[5]. The following two roles are defined in addition:

$\qquad$ lonAligned $\equiv$ northAlignedWith ⊔ southAlignedWith
$\qquad$ latAligned $\equiv$ eastAlignedWith ⊔ westAlignedWith ,

lon and lat being shortcuts for longitudinal and lateral. In contrast to their defining base relations, these relations are symmetric.

Recall from the symbol grounding for SceneObjects (Sec. 5.1.1), that a triple of individuals Road $\xrightarrow{\text{lonAligned}}$ RoadTransition $\xrightarrow{\text{lonAligned}}$ Road, as well as Lane $\xrightarrow{\text{lonAligned}}$ LaneTransition $\xrightarrow{\text{lonAligned}}$ Lane indicates a *driveable path* from one Road|Lane to the other.

Spatial Neighbourhood

A particularity of the intersection domain is that the types of aligned SceneObjects frequently alternates, both in lateral (e.g. lane, divider, lane, divider, ...) and longitudinal (road, road transition, road, road transition, ...) direction. The second composed descriptor $\mathcal{T}_{Neighbourhood}$ describes such pairs of elements of identical type, which are not spatially connected to each other, but are next but one elements in a chain of {lon | lat}Aligned primitives. This symmetric descriptor is defined by the following TBox:

---

[5]The notAligned role, which is provided here to ensure the descriptors' JEPD property, was not implemented in RONNY for computational reasons.

$\mathcal{T}_{Neighbourhood} = \{$
   neighbourRelation $\sqsubseteq$ spatialRelation ,
   neighbourRelation $\equiv$ lonNeighbour ⊔ latNeighbour⊔
                        noNeighbour ,
   lonNeighbour $\equiv$ neighbourRelation ⊓ dc ⊓
                  lonAligned ○ lonAligned ,
   latNeighbour $\equiv$ neighbourRelation ⊓ dc ⊓
                  latAligned ○ latAligned ,
   noNeighbour $\equiv$ neighbourRelation ⊓
                  ¬latNeighbour ⊓ ¬lonNeighbour ,
   $\underline{C}_1$ $\sqsubseteq \forall$neighbourRelation.$\underline{C}_1$,
   ...
   $\underline{C}_n$ $\sqsubseteq \forall$neighbourRelation.$\underline{C}_n$
$\}$.

The placeholders $\underline{C}_i$ refer to set of **SceneObject**s which are in the domain of neighbourRelation, namely **Lane** and **Road** here. The dc role is needed in the definitions to ensure that individuals do not become *Neighbours of themselves. This set of definitions is approximated via rules in the implementation.

Relative Heading

The descriptor $\mathcal{T}_{RelHeading}$ describes possible headings of an individual ind_j that is northAlignedWith the reference individual ind_i. It refers to the relative tangent orientation of ind_j at the point farthest away from ind_i.

$\mathcal{T}_{RelHeading} = \{$
   headingRelation $\sqsubseteq$ spatialRelation ,
   headingRelation $\equiv$ headingStraightAhead ⊔ headingEastwards⊔
                   headingWestwards ⊔ headingBackwards ⊔
                   noHeading $\}$

Let γ denote the angle difference between the tangent at end point of the first operand, $\mathbf{p}_{e,1}$, and the tangent at that point $\mathbf{p} \in \{\mathbf{p}_{s,2}, \mathbf{p}_{e,2}\}$ of the second operand with the larger distance to $\mathbf{p}_{e,1}$. Then the relHeading base relations are grounded

5.1. SYMBOL GROUNDING

as follows:

$$(ind_i, ind_j) : \begin{cases} \text{headingStraightAhead} & , \text{northAlignedWith} \wedge \\ & \gamma \in [-45°, 45°) \\ \text{headingEastwards} & , \text{northAlignedWith} \wedge \\ & \gamma \in [45°, 170°) \\ \text{headingBackwards} & , \text{northAlignedWith} \wedge \\ & \gamma \in [170°, 190°) \\ \text{headingWestwards} & , \text{northAlignedWith} \wedge \\ & \gamma \in [190°, 315°) \\ \text{noHeading} & , \text{otherwise} \end{cases}$$

Figure 5.5 summarises the taxonomy of spatial relations implemented in RONNY.

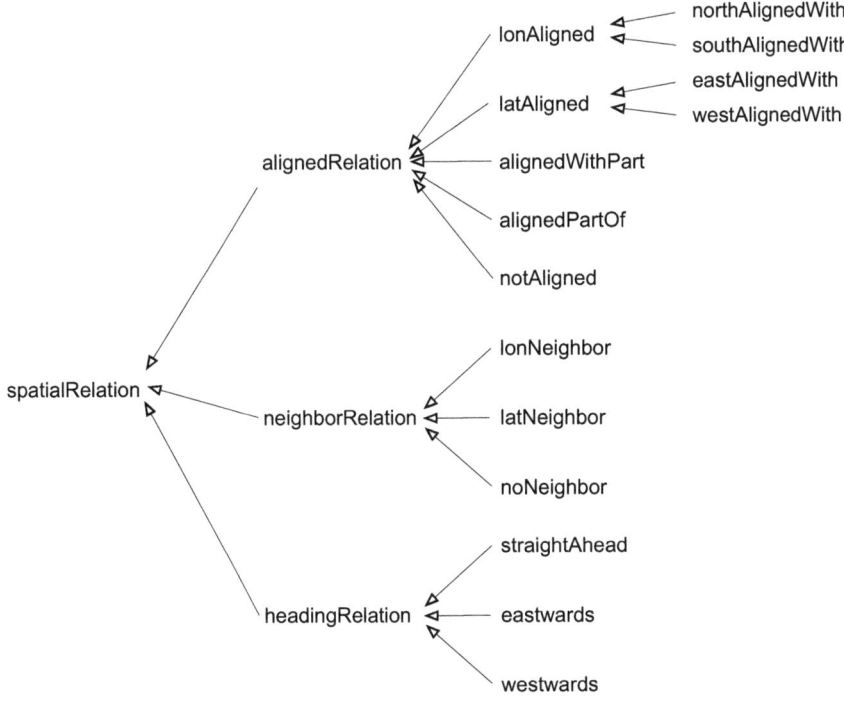

Figure 5.5: **Taxonomy of** spatialRelations.

ABox requirements

For complete reasoning with respect to spatial relations, RONNY adopts the approximation to JEPD semantics for relations proposed in Section 4.2.2. As outlined there, the approximation requires an ABox which is complete with respect to the implemented descriptors, i. e. $\mathcal{T}_{Alignedness}$ and $\mathcal{T}_{Neighbourhood}$ and $\mathcal{T}_{RelHeading}$, for ClosedWorldConcepts. Checking an ABox for completeness can be done using Pattern ABOX_CHECK (Section 4.2.2):

$x_2 : \bot \Leftarrow x_1 :$ ClosedWorldConcept $\wedge$ neg$((x_1, x_2) :$ alignedRelation$)$
$x_2 : \bot \Leftarrow x_1 :$ ClosedWorldConcept $\wedge$ neg$((x_1, x_2) :$ neighbourRelation$)$
$x_2 : \bot \Leftarrow x_1 :$ ClosedWorldConcept $\wedge$ neg$((x_1, x_2) :$ headingRelation$)$.

In Computer Vision terms, this requires to compute the correct **degreeOfOverlap**, **relPosition**, and **relOrientation** relation for each pair of detected objects. Therefrom the base relations of the implemented descriptors are then derivable with the provided role definitions.

As the neighbourRelations are exhaustively defined out of alignedRelations, completeness of either $\mathcal{T}_{Alignedness}$ or $\mathcal{T}_{Neighbourhood}$ suffices in theory. However, as in the implementation these definitions are only approximated by means of trigger rules, reasoning will not be complete in this case.

When this prerequisite is met, Design Pattern SPATIAL_CLOSURE (Section 4.2.2) can be instantiated as required:

$\mathcal{T}_{SPATIAL\_CLOSURE} = \{$
    spatialRelation $\sqsubseteq$ closedWorldRole   ,
    alignedRelation $\sqsubseteq$ spatialRelation   ,
    neighbourRelation $\sqsubseteq$ spatialRelation   ,
    headingRelation $\sqsubseteq$ spatialRelation $\}$.

With this set of axioms, the procedural extension of RONNY will be extended by the closure assertions required to approximate JEPD semantics for the implemented spatial descriptors.

5.1.4 Taxonomy of **Functionality** and **functionalRelation**s

In addition to SceneObjects, which were defined as objects potentially physically present in the considered scene, RONNY also contains a class Functionality,

5.1. SYMBOL GROUNDING

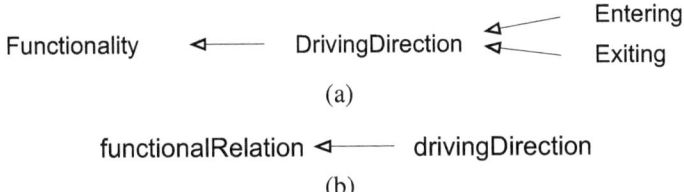

Figure 5.6: *(a)* **Taxonomy of** Functionality **Primitives,** *(b)* **Taxonomy of** functionalRelations.

which is disjoint from SceneObject. At present, it comprises only one concept DrivingDirection.

These primitives are grounded as follows:

Functionality   Subsumes concepts that describe functional properties of SceneObjects. They are no SceneObjects and therefore do not possess geometrical properties.

DrivingDirection   Describes the allowed directions of travel on Lane and Road individuals with respect to the egocentric frame. Since at present, however, all egocentric frames point towards the junction by convention (cf. Sec. 5.1.2), directions of travel are described directly relative to the junction, omitting one coordinate transformation. Its subclasses Entering and Exiting are not disjoint, as individuals may allow for both.

The role drivingDirection has domain Road ⊔ Lane and range DrivingDirection.

5.1.5 Defined Concepts

In the previous sections, a set of *primitive concepts* and roles was introduced, and each primitive was grounded by providing a description of its corresponding entity in the real world. Next a set of further useful concepts will be defined (by using the $\equiv$-constructor[6]) out of these primitives. They are called *defined concepts* and can be regarded as abbreviations of longer concept descriptions. They will prove useful for providing compact descriptions of the road building regulations later on.

---

[6]Some of the definitions contain role conjuncts, which are not supported in $\mathcal{SHIQ}$. They are approximated using rules in the implementation.

$\mathcal{T}_{Defineables} = \{$

// one way := either a one way entering or a one way exiting (see below).
OneWay $\equiv$ OneWayEntering $\sqcup$ OneWayExiting ,

// one way entering/exiting := a lane or a road, which permits driving
// towards/away from the junction only.
OneWayEntering $\equiv$ (Lane $\sqcup$ Road) $\sqcap$ $\forall$drivingDirection.Entering ,
OneWayExiting $\equiv$ (Lane $\sqcup$ Road) $\sqcap$ $\forall$drivingDirection.Exiting ,

// turning lane := either a right turn or a straight ahead or a
// left turn lane. It has a driving direction towards the junction.
TurningLane $\equiv$ RightTurnLane $\sqcup$ StraightAheadLane $\sqcup$ LeftTurnLane ,
TurningLane $\sqsubseteq$ $\exists$hasDrivingDirection.Entering ,

// right turn lane := a turning lane which is longitudinally aligned
// with some lane transition heading eastwards.
RightTurnLane $\equiv$ TurningLane $\sqcap$ $\exists$headingEastwards.LaneTransition ,

// straight ahead lane := a turning lane which is longitudinally aligned
// with some lane transition leading straight ahead.
StraightAheadLane $\equiv$ TurningLane $\sqcap$ $\exists$headingStraightAhead.LaneTransition ,

// left turn lane := a turning lane which is longitudinally aligned
// with some lane transition heading westwards.
LeftTurnLane $\equiv$ TurningLane $\sqcap$ $\exists$headingWestwards.LaneTransition ,

// outermost lane := a lane, which has at most one lateral neighbour.
OutermostLane $\equiv$ Lane $\sqcap$ $\exists_{\leq 1}$latNeighbour.$\top$

$\}$.

The set of introduced primitives and defineables constitutes RONNY's *vocabulary* for the intersection domain.

5.2 Intersection Geometry Model

A qualitative model of intersection geometry consists of a) a set of constraints on the geometry of SceneObjects, and b) a set of constraints for the spatialRelations that are allowed to hold between them (see Section 4.2). Both sets of constraints are axiomatised below using the introduced vocabulary for the intersection domain. The set of ABoxes that is consistent with respect to these constraints spans the hypothesis space of qualitative intersection geometries.

5.2.1 Object Geometry

Each SceneObject for which qualitative geometry shall be modelled or inferred, must inherit from concept GeometricEntity. In the previous section, Pattern OBJECT_GEOMETRY was instantiated with the three classes of GeometricEntity descendants termed GP1, GP2 and GP3. The admissible geometries of a SceneObject ⊓ GeometricEntity concept are constrained by making it a descendant of only a subset of GPis.

RONNY models the geometry of its SceneObjects as follows: Roads and lanes outside of junctions are always of shape GP1. Lanes on the junction (LaneTransitions) can be of any of the introduced shapes. Due to their lateral alignment, the same must hold for dividers. Road transitions (consisting of several lane transitions) and junctions (consisting of several road transitions) have complex shapes and therefore are not GeometricPrimitives anymore. These specifications translate into DL as:

$$
\begin{aligned}
\mathcal{T}_{ObjGeo} \supset \{ & \\
\text{Road} & \sqsubseteq \text{GP1}, \\
\text{Lane} & \sqsubseteq \text{GP1}, \\
\text{RoadTransition} & \sqsubseteq \text{GeometricEntity}, \\
\text{LaneTransition} & \sqsubseteq \text{GP1} \sqcup \text{GP2} \sqcup \text{GP3}, \\
\text{Divider} & \sqsubseteq \text{GP1} \sqcup \text{GP2} \sqcup \text{GP3}, \\
\text{Junction} & \sqsubseteq \text{GeometricEntity} \quad \}.
\end{aligned}
$$

5.2.2 Scene Geometry

Relational scene geometry is modelled by providing constraints for the spatialRelations that are allowed to hold between the GeometricEntity concepts.

88 5. RONNY: THE ROAD NETWORK ONTOLOGY

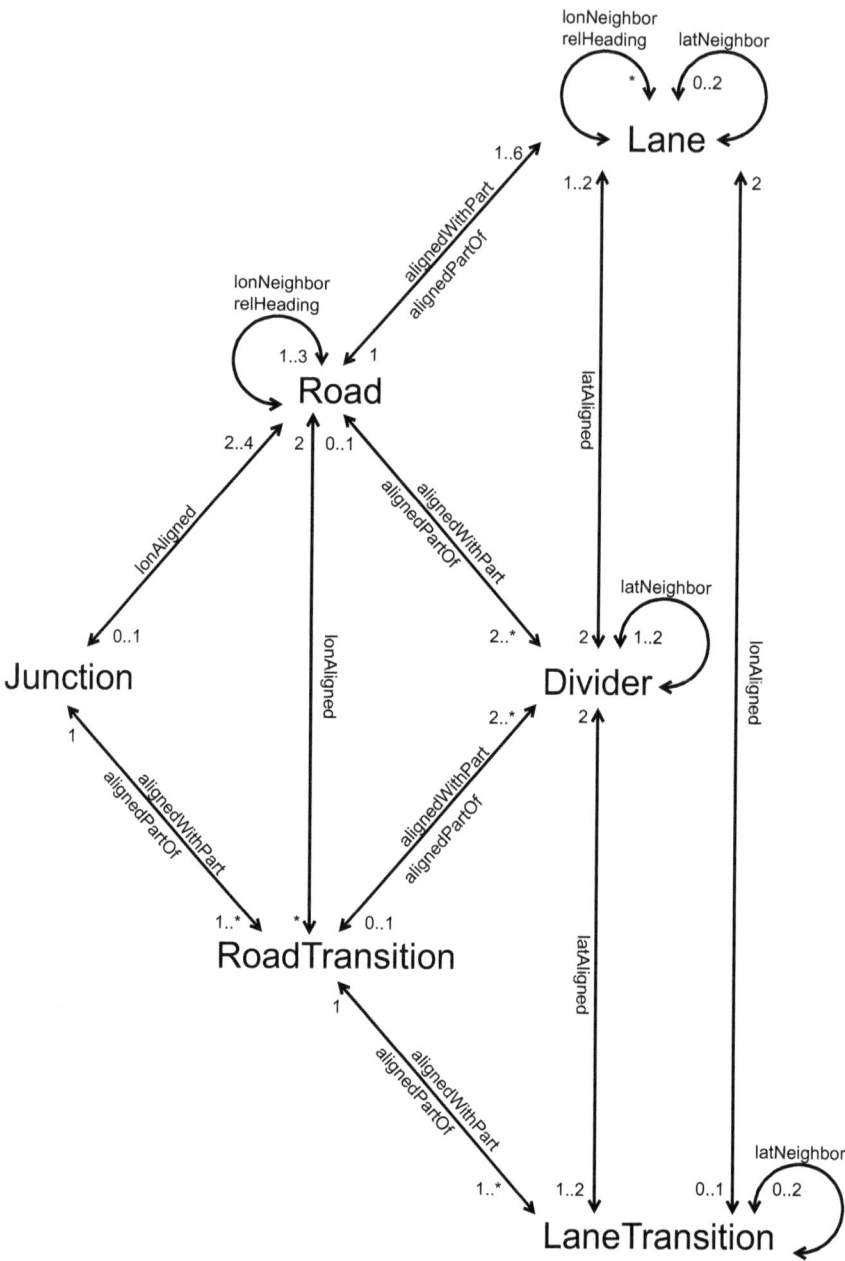

Figure 5.7: **Qualitative Geometry Model for Intersections.**

They are specified graphically using the nomenclature defined in Figure 4.2 (Section 4.2.3). Its unique mapping into the DL $\mathcal{SHIQ}$ is given by the corresponding Pattern SCENE_GEOMETRY.

RONNY's model for relational intersection geometry is depicted in Figure 5.7. The graphical specification contains all allowed base relations with respect to the $\mathcal{T}_{Alignedness}$, $\mathcal{T}_{Neighbourhood}$ and $\mathcal{T}_{RelHeading}$ descriptors. The set of depicted concepts covers the GeometricEntity concept. The roles notAligned and noNeighbour were omitted, as well as the transitive hull for alignedWithPart and its inverse, for better readability. Always, the highest possible concept abstraction was chosen, i.e. if the spatial relations are identical for all children of a covered concept, then the superconcept is used.

A rough textual description of the RONNY scene model reads as follows: A road has one to six lanes and a couple of dividers as aligned parts. Each of its lanes is aligned laterally with two of its dividers. Pairs of lanes laterally aligned with the same divider are lateral neighbours. A road can be longitudinally aligned with road transitions only. Two roads aligned with a common road transition are longitudinal neighbours. The analogue is true for lanes. A set of road transitions, the roads of which are pairwise longitudinal neighbours, constitutes a junction. Consequently, in the case of only two neighbouring roads, already a single road transition classifies as a junction. For computational reasons, RONNY allows at most one junction per ABox (which is enforced using a rule). For the same reason, longitudinal alignedness of Junctions is only modelled where relevant (it has been omitted between junctions and lanes, and between roads and lanes). Also, the relative heading between individuals is modelled only among roads and among lanes. Arbitrary headings are allowed there.

The formalisation of these constraints restricts the hypothesis space of qualitative intersection geometries. Only those ABoxes which do not violate any constraint will be classified consistent with respect to the RONNY TBox.

5.3 Road Building Regulations

Up to now, a vocabulary for the intersection domain has been set up, consisting of primitive SceneObject and Functionality concepts, of primitive spatialRelations and functionalRelations, and of some defined concepts. It has been used in the previous Section for setting up a hypothesis space of admissible qualitative scene geometries. In this section, this vocabulary will be used to formulate high-level road building regulations. Semantic as well as high-level geometric building regulations will be axiomatised. These regulations will serve as yet another set of constraints on the set of admissible intersections.

The road building regulations formulated in the following are tailored to *German* road networks[7]. Other countries may differ in the set of admissible road layouts, in the semantics of marking types, and so on. To adapt the RONNY TBox to another country, any Germany-specific regulation can be removed or replaced by other axioms. This exhibits a very strong benefit of KR languages which are explicit, declarative, and modular.

Within this geographic limitation, the regulations formulated are intended to be of *general validity*. It can, however, not be excluded that a German road exists that violates one of the assumptions. Their validity will be tested in the next chapter on a set of complex urban intersections.

5.3.1 Right-handed Traffic

Right- and left-handed traffic differ in the lateral arrangement of driving directions on a road. Furthermore, they have a reversed arrangement of turning lanes on the road: For right-handed traffic, right turn lanes are (geometrically) equal to / east of straight ahead lanes, which are equal to / east of left turn lanes, while the reverse is true for left-handed traffic ("equal to" denotes that these three turning lanes are not necessarily disjoint, i. e. a lane might be a straight ahead lane *and* a right turn lane). These constraints are axiomatised for right-handed traffic below. Exchanging them with their left-handed traffic equivalents yields an Intersection Understanding system for left-handed traffic instead.

$\mathcal{T}_{RightHandedTraffic} = \{$

// East neighbours of lanes/roads entering the junction enter the junction.
// West neighbours of lanes/roads exiting the junction exit the junction.

∃drivingDirection.
Entering   ⊑ ∀eastNeighbour.(∃drivingDirection.Entering) ,
∃drivingDirection.
Exiting   ⊑ ∀westNeighbour.(∃drivingDirection.Exiting)   ,

// East neighbours of right turn lanes always are right turn lanes.
RightTurnLane   ⊑ ∀eastNeighbour.¬(StraightAheadLane ⊔
                    LeftTurnLane)   ,

---

[7]Originally, an attempt had been made to derive the regulations from official road building guidelines, such as the "Recommendations for the design of inner-city roads" (RASt 2007). It turned out, however, that on one hand many common-sense regulations were not contained in these works, and that on the other hand many of the regulations contained were not relevant with respect to the vocabulary introduced here. Consequently the building regulations formulated in the following are not derived from official guidelines but from common-sense reflections.

5.3. Road Building Regulations

// East neighbours of straight ahead lanes are never left turn lanes.
// West neighbours of straight ahead lanes are never right turn lanes.
StraightAheadLane ⊑ ∀eastNeighbour.¬LeftTurnLane ⊓
                ∀westNeighbour.¬(StraightAheadLane ⊔
                RightTurnLane)   ,

// West neighbours of left turn lanes are never straight ahead or
// right turn lanes.
LeftTurnLane   ⊑ ∀westNeighbour.¬(StraightAheadLane ⊔
                RightTurnLane)   } .

Note that drivingDirection and {east|west}Neighbour relations, as well as the three defined TurningLane classes, operate in the egocentric frame of the referred road which is assumed pointing towards the junction (see Sec. 5.1.2).

5.3.2 Dividers

Dividers visually mark the lateral borders of a lane. Additionally, their type indicates, among other things, which type of traffic participant is permitted on a lane. Information about permitted traffic participants is modelled in RONNY by the three lane subclasses MotorVehLane, BicycleLane and EmergencyLane. The following inclusion axioms constrain these subclasses according to the type of divider they are laterally aligned with. Confer Section 5.1 for reference to the respective Divider subclasses and their grounding.

$\mathcal{T}_{Dividers} = \{$
  // A dashed, 12cm wide divider is aligned with two car lanes.
  Dashed ⊓ 12cm ⊑ ∃$_{=2}$ latAligned.MotorVehLane   ,
  // A dashed, 25cm divider is aligned with a bicycle-only and a car lane.
  Dashed ⊓ 25cm ⊑ ∃latAligned.(BicycleLane ⊓ ¬MotorVehLane) ⊓
                  ∃latAligned.MotorVehLane   ,
  // A 12cm wide solid or a physical divider is aligned with the road's
  // outermost lane (road borders), or with two lanes with different
  // driving directions (road centerline).
  (Solid ⊓ 12cm)
    ⊔ Physical   ⊑ ∃$_{\leq 1}$ latAligned.OneWayEntering ⊓
                ∃$_{\leq 1}$ latAligned.OneWayExiting   ,

// A solid, 25cm wide divider is aligned with a car lane and an emergency
// or bicycle-only lane.
Solid ⊓ 25cm ⊑ ∃latAligned.MotorVehLane ⊓
          ∃latAligned.((BicycleLane ⊓ ¬MotorVehLane)
          ⊔ EmergencyLane)
} .

Recall from their symbol grounding that **MotorVehLane** and **BicycleLane** are not disjoint. Therefore, lanes which are exclusively for one type of traffic participant need to be modelled as e. g. **BicycleLane** ⊓ ¬**MotorVehLane**, for a *bicycles-only* lane.

5.3.3 Driving Directions

Driving directions are restricted by the constraints for right-handed traffic and by the definition for **OneWay**s (Sec. 5.1.5). Only few more axioms are required.

$\mathcal{T}_{DrivingDirections} = \{$
// A road allows for a driving direction, iff ≥ 1 of its lanes allows for it.
Road ⊓
∃drivingDirection.Entering ≡ Road ⊓ ∃alignedWithPart.
                              (Lane ⊓ ∃drivingDirection.Entering) ,
Road ⊓
∃drivingDirection.Exiting ≡ Road ⊓ ∃alignedWithPart.
                              (Lane ⊓ ∃drivingDirection.Exiting) ,
// A road containing more than one lane does not contain two-way lanes.
Road ⊓
∃$_{\geq 2}$ alignedWithPart.Lane ⊑ ¬∃alignedWithPart.TwoWay ,
// A Freeway is a one way road.
Freeway   ⊑ OneWay
} .

5.3.4 Bicycle/Car/Emergency Lanes

In addition to the preceding axioms, the presence and the amount of **BicycleLane**s, **EmergencyLane**s, and **MotorVehLane**s is further constrained

5.3. ROAD BUILDING REGULATIONS

by the following set of axioms:

$\mathcal{T}_{LaneTypes} = \{$

// A road has at least one car lane per driving direction.
Road ⊓
∃drivingDirection.Entering ⊑ ∃alignedWithPart.(MotorVehLane ⊓
 ∃drivingDirection.Entering) ,
Road ⊓
∃drivingDirection.Exiting ⊑ ∃alignedWithPart.(MotorVehLane ⊓ ,
 ∃drivingDirection.Exiting) ,

// A road has at most one bicycle lane per driving direction.
Road   ⊑ ∃$_{\leq 1}$ alignedWithPart.(BicycleLane ⊓ ,
 ∃drivingDirection.Entering) ,
Road   ⊑ ∃$_{\leq 1}$ alignedWithPart.(BicycleLane ⊓ ,
 ∃drivingDirection.Exiting) ,

// Bicycles are not allowed on freeways and highways. Emergency
// lanes are only required on freeways and highways.
Freeway   ⊑ ∀alignedWithPart. ¬BicycleLane   ,
Highway   ⊑ ∀alignedWithPart. ¬BicycleLane   ,
UrbanRoad   ⊑ ∀alignedWithPart. ¬EmergencyLane ,

// An emergency lane is the outermost lane of a road.
EmergencyLane   ⊑ OutermostLane   ,

// Bicycle lanes of a given turning lane type are always the eastmost lane
// of that turning lane type.
BicycleLane ⊓
RightTurnLane   ⊑ ¬∃eastNeighbour.RightTurnLane   ,
BicycleLane ⊓
StraightAheadLane   ⊑ ¬∃eastNeighbour.StraightAheadLane ,
BicycleLane ⊓
LeftTurnLane   ⊑ ¬∃eastNeighbour.LeftTurnLane
$\}$.

The first axiom ensures that only networks designated for cars are dealt with. Bicycle-only roads, for example, are ruled out. Confer Section 5.1 for a precise grounding of the mentioned Lane subclasses.

5.3.5 Driveable Paths

The notion of a *driveable path* between roads has been defined in Section 5.1.1 as a triple of Road $\xrightarrow{\text{lonAligned}}$ RoadTransition $\xrightarrow{\text{lonAligned}}$ Road individuals. Such a driveable path exists iff there is at least one triple of Lane $\xrightarrow{\text{lonAligned}}$ LaneTransition $\xrightarrow{\text{lonAligned}}$ individuals, which are part of these road(transition)s. Such a LaneTransition is present between two Lanes, iff one is reachable from the other *without performing a lane change*.

The fact that a RoadTransition requires at least one LaneTransition to be part of it, has already been axiomatised in the geometry model. The following set of axioms are required in addition:

$\mathcal{T}_{Paths} = \{$

// *No isolated roads:*
// *A road that connects to a junction has some driveable path.*
Road ⊓
∃lonAligned.Junction ⊑ ∃lonAligned.RoadTransition

// *No isolated lanes:*
// *A lane that connects to a junction has some driveable path.*
Lane ⊓
∃lonAligned.Junction ⊑ ∃lonAligned.LaneTransition

// *No opposing flow of traffic:*
// *A driveable path between lanes requires entering and exiting traffic flow.*
LaneTransition ⊑ ∃lonAligned.(∃drivingDirection.Entering) ⊓
∃lonAligned.(∃drivingDirection.Exiting) ,

// *No lane change:*
// *A lane has max. 1 driveable path leading {eastwards|westwards}.*
// *A lane has max. 2 driveable paths leading straight ahead*
// *(this accounts for widening/narrowing of straight ahead lanes).*
Lane   ⊑ ∃$_{\leq 1}$headingEastwards.LaneTransition   ,
Lane   ⊑ ∃$_{\leq 1}$headingWestwards.LaneTransition   ,
Lane   ⊑ ∃$_{\leq 2}$headingStraightAhead.LaneTransition
$\}$.

Note that, to fully account for the definition of a driveable path, two further constraints would be required here: A RoadTransition may be lonAligned only to those Roads, which are lonAligned to that particular Junction that it belongs to. Similarly, a RoadTransition may only contain LaneTransitions which are

IonAligned to Lanes, that are part of those Roads that the RoadTransition is IonAligned to. These constraints are only axiomatisable using role chains, which are not available in $\mathcal{SHIQ}$. Therefore, they must be ensured on the ABox side.

5.3.6 Geometry of Paths

The geometry of a driveable path is determined by the geometry of the involved SceneObjects. Recall from the object geometry modelling in Section 5.2.1 that Roads and Lanes are always of shape GP1, whereas LaneTransitions can be of any of the introduced shapes. Therefore, the path geometry is determined by the type of primitive, GP1, GP2 or GP3, of the LaneTransition. It is constrained as follows:

$\mathcal{T}_{PathGeometry} = \{$
   // *A lane transition leading east- or westwards is of shape GP3.*
   // *A lane transition leading straight ahead is of shape GP1 or GP2.*
   Lane $\sqsubseteq$ ∀headingEastwards.(GP3 ⊔ ¬LaneTransition) ,
   Lane $\sqsubseteq$ ∀headingWestwards.(GP3 ⊔ ¬LaneTransition) ,
   Lane $\sqsubseteq$ ∀headingStraightAhead.(GP1 ⊔ GP2 ⊔ ¬LaneTransition) ,

   // *A lane entering a GP2 transition always enters a GP1 transition, too.*
   OneWayEntering ⊓ ∃IonAligned.GP2 $\sqsubseteq$ ∃IonAligned.GP1 ,

   // *A lane transition of shape GP2 is present only on junctions without*
   // *crossing roads.*
   Lane ⊓ ∃headingEastwards) $\sqsubseteq$ ¬∃IonAligned.GP2 ,
   Lane ⊓ ∃(headingWestwards) $\sqsubseteq$ ¬∃IonAligned.GP2 ,

   // *Only outermost car lanes can lead to a GP2 lane transition.*
   ¬OutermostCarLane $\sqsubseteq$ ¬∃IonAligned.GP2 ,

   // *A freeway contains straight ahead lanes only (due to its small*
   // *curvature, even on slip roads).*
   Freeway $\sqsubseteq$ ¬∃alignedWithPart.(∃IonAligned.GP3)
$\}$.

It is vital to note that RONNY's axiom set is not required to be complete to produce correct reasoning results. On the contrary, some road building regulations are certainly not covered by the set of provided axioms. As deduction infers only *provable* statements, no false statements are ever produced. In classification terms, an individual may remain unclassified, but no false positives or negatives will ever be produced given that the sensor data is correct. False positives, false negatives, and ABox inconsistencies indicate a TBox modelling error.

6 Application: DL-based Intersection Understanding

The MRT lab owns two experimental vehicles, which are equipped with a variety of external and internal sensors and actuators for autonomous driving. Three of its sensors, a stereo vision sensor, a digital map, and a global positioning system (GPS), were used for conducting the set of experiments subsequently described.

Section 6.1 describes the characteristics of each sensor and the mapping of its data into a RONNY ABox, based on a particular intersection example. This allows for the automatic creation of ABoxes out of sensor data, their transmission to the reasoner using RACERPRO's TCP interface, and subsequent Scene Interpretation reasoning on the basis of the RONNY TBox.

Figure 6.1: MRT Autonomous Vehicle "AnnieWay". For a detailed description of the AnnieWay project, see e. g. (Kammel et al. 2008).

Section 6.2 describes a sample set of real-world intersections, and Section 6.3 provides a quantitative evaluation of a set of reasoning experiments on this sample set. The tasks addressed are object detection, object classification, and data association in the context of intersection interpretation.

For better readability, the following naming scheme for individuals will be used uniformly throughout this chapter:

r_i	Road individual
l_{ij}	Lane individual that is alignedPartOf road r_i
$tr\text{-}r_i\text{-}r_j$	TransitionRoad individual lonAligned with roads r_i and r_j
$tr\text{-}l_{im}\text{-}l_{jn}$	TransitionLane lonAligned with lanes l_{im} and l_{jn}
d_i	Divider individual

6.1 Sensor Setup

A digital map, a camera and an absolute positioning device are used as sensor input. As will be described later, all three sensors deliver *objects* (as opposed to sets of features, cf. Sec. 4.1.2), like e. g. Lanes or Dividers. Furthermore, the sensor setup is *redundant*, as for example a Lane can potentially be detected by all three sensors. This setup is axiomatised by instantiating the TBox in Design Pattern SENSOR_SETUP (Section 4.1.2) as follows:

$\mathcal{T}_{SENSOR\_SETUP} = \{$
  SensorInput $\equiv$ MapInput $\sqcup$ CameraInput $\sqcup$ GPSInput ,
  MapInput $\sqsubseteq$ SceneObject ,
  CameraInput $\sqsubseteq$ SceneObject ,
  GPSInput $\sqsubseteq$ SceneObject ,
  // For the set of complementary sensors $\{i,..,j\}, i,j \in \{1,..,n\}$, add:
  // disjoint(SensorInput$_i$,...,SensorInput$_j$)
$\}$

Furthermore, the map delivers the *complete* set of Roads, Lanes and Junctions (this will be described in the next Subsection). To exploit this important feature, Design Pattern LOCALLY_CLOSED_WORLD (Section 4.1.1) needs to be instantiated:

$\mathcal{T}_{LOCALLY\_CLOSED\_WORLD} = \{$
  Road $\sqsubseteq$ ClosedWorldConcept ,
  Lane $\sqsubseteq$ ClosedWorldConcept $\}$.
  Junction $\sqsubseteq$ ClosedWorldConcept $\}$.

The ABox assertions required by both patterns are added automatically through the procedural extension given in Algorithm 2.

Note that all spatial relations are required to be closed with respect to ClosedWorldConcepts (see Sec. 5.1.3). This implies that the aligned- and headingRelation must be given for each individual with respect to the subset of Road $\sqcup$ Lane $\sqcup$ Junction individuals. In Computer Vision terms: New individuals can only be delivered by an *extrinsically calibrated* sensor, the position accuracy of which must be within lane-precision. A way to proceed if this data is unavailable, as is the case for the vision sensor in this setting, is sketched in Section 6.1.3.

6.1. SENSOR SETUP

This set of axioms completes the RONNY TBox. Next, using a particular intersection example, a RONNY ABox for an example intersection will be given for each sensory input.

6.1.1 Digital Map

The map is an off-the-shelf product from TeleAtlas, developed for car navigation systems. For this reason, it accurately captures road network topology, i.e. the connectivity between roads, whereas network geometry is only coarsely digitised. Roads are represented by geographic (latitude, longitude) start and end coordinate pairs, junctions by one coordinate pair only. The geographic coordinates are transformed into RONNY's metric UTM frame (cf. Sec. 5.1.2) using the UTM projection. The following further attributes are provided by the map:

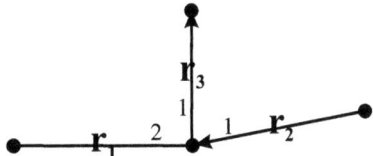

Figure 6.2: **Digital Map** Example for a junction connecting to 3 roads. The number of lanes and the permitted driving directions are visualised (a lacking arrow head indicates a two-way road).

Each road's allowed driving directions $\in$ {OneWayNorth, OneWaySouth, TwoWay}, and its road class $\in$ {Freeway,...,PedestrianMall}. Lanes are not yet contained in the map. More recently deployed so-called ADAS (advanced driver assistance systems) maps also contain the number of lanes per road. This information was provided manually in addition.

Axiomatisation of Detections

As axiomatised above, all roads and lanes at the considered junction require instantiation in RONNY. For the example from Figure 6.2:

$\mathcal{A}_{Map, Detections} = \{$
$\quad j_1 \; : \mathsf{MapInput} \sqcap \mathsf{Junction} \quad ,$
$\quad r_1 \; : \mathsf{MapInput} \sqcap \mathsf{Road} \quad ,$
$\quad r_2 \; : \mathsf{MapInput} \sqcap \mathsf{Road} \quad ,$
$\quad r_3 \; : \mathsf{MapInput} \sqcap \mathsf{Road} \quad ,$
$\quad l_{11} : \mathsf{MapInput} \sqcap \mathsf{Lane} \quad ,$
$\quad l_{12} : \mathsf{MapInput} \sqcap \mathsf{Lane} \quad ,$
$\quad l_{21} : \mathsf{MapInput} \sqcap \mathsf{Lane} \quad ,$

l_{31} : MapInput ⊓ Lane   } .

MapInput states that the individual has been provided by the map sensor (as required by Pattern SENSOR_SETUP). Additionally, the set of Dividers could be instantiated without loss of generality (a missing divider can later be classified InvisibleDivider). This has been omitted here to keep the example simple. Dividers are thus ¬ClosedWorldConcepts.

Axiomatisation of Classifications

The map's driving direction information maps to the defined concepts OneWayEntering, OneWayExiting, and ¬OneWay (cf. Sec. 5.1.5), all specified relative to the junction. The road classes are mapped to the three Road descendants Freeway, CountryRoad and UrbanRoad. The example translates to RONNY as:

$\mathcal{A}_{Map, Classifications} = \{$
   r_1 : ¬OneWay   ,
   r_2 : OneWayEntering ,
   r_3 : OneWayExiting   ,
   r_1 : UrbanRoad   ,
   r_2 : UrbanRoad   ,
   r_3 : UrbanRoad   } .

Axiomatisation of Spatial Relations

As mentioned, all alignedRelations and headingRelations need to be stated for the ClosedWorldConcept descendants (Sec. 6.1). The following relations hold for road r_1:

$\mathcal{A}_{Map, Alignedness} = \{$
   (r_1, j_1) : IonAligned   ,
   (r_1, l_{11}) : alignedWithPart ,
   (r_1, l_{12}) : alignedWithPart ,

   (r_1, r_2) : headingStraightAhead ,
   (r_1, r_3) : headingWestwards   } .

For the definition of these relations see Section 5.1.3. The relations for roads r_2 and r_3 are formulated analogously. The following rule must be supplemented for automatic provision of all notAligned relations:

   (x_1, x_2) : notAligned ⇐
   x_1 : ClosedWorldConcept ∧ neg$((x_1, x_2)$: AlignedRelation$)$.

6.1. SENSOR SETUP

It asserts notAligned to all individual pairs which do not have a $\mathcal{T}_{Alignedness}$ relation yet. Due to its non-monotonic nature (cf. Sec. 3.4), this rule must be executed *after* all other alignedRelations have been stated.

Axiomatising Driveable Path Hypotheses

The map accurately provides road-level connectivity, but lacks a description of the connectivity on the junction. In particular: Which road has a *driveable path* (RONNY's RoadTransitions) to which other road? Which of its lanes has such a driveable path (RONNY's LaneTransitions)? What does the qualitative geometry (RONNY's GeometricPrimitives) of the paths look like?

The reasoning service should be able to infer from the previous ABox assertions and RONNY's axioms about driveable paths (Sec. 5.3.5), that a Road which is lonAligned to a Junction must be lonAligned to some of its RoadTransitions, create the provably existent transitions, and assert the required relations. This kind of reasoning was introduced as "object detection reasoning" in Section 4.3.1. Instantiating the corresponding Pattern OBJECT_DETECTION for this task yields:

$$\mathcal{T}_{OBJECT\_DETECTION} = \{$$
  ObjectHypothesis $\equiv$ Verified $\sqcup$ Falsified ,
  disjoint(Verified, Falsified) ,
  ObjectHypothesis $\sqsubseteq$ ClosedWorldConcept ,
  RoadTransition $\sqsubseteq$ Verified
$\}$.

$$\mathcal{A}_{OBJECT\_DETECTION} = \{$$
  tr-r_1-r_2 : ObjectHypothesis ,
  $(tr$-r_1-$r_2,\ j_1)$: alignedPartOf ,
  $(tr$-r_1-$r_2,\ r_1)$: lonAligned ,
  $(tr$-r_1-$r_2,\ r_2)$: lonAligned $\}$.

It states that the term RoadTransition refers to a verified object hypothesis, that all object hypothesis individuals are introduced, and that individual tr-r_1-r_2 is an hypothesis. Analogous ABox assertions are required for the other two hypothetically possible transitions tr-r_1-r_3 and tr-r_2-r_3 (one transition per pair of roads aligned with the junction, order irrelevant). Each can either be verified or falsified. Only a Verified individual can be a RoadTransition. Likewise, the template is also instantiated for all potential LaneTransitions. In the implementation, $\mathcal{A}_{OBJECT\_DETECTION}$ is supplemented automatically for {Road|Lane}Transitions by means of rules. Note that the model of scene geometry (cf. Sec. 5.2.2) must be modified to additionally allow for an ObjectHypothesis whenever allowing for a *Transition in its domain constraints.

This axiomatisation enables reasoning about the existence and the geometry of {Road|Lane}Transitions, as will be demonstrated in the experiments.

6.1.2 Positioning Sensor and Map Matching

A reliable vehicle pose estimate is required not only for navigation purposes, but also for relating global, map-based information to local, e. g. video-based, data. The MRT's experimental vehicles are equipped with global positioning devices (GPS) for estimating vehicle pose, i. e. position and heading in geographic coordinates, and speed. However, multipath effects in urban areas cause positional standard deviations of 15m/5m for standard/differential GPS. Inertial sensors, that is motion sensing devices like accelerometers or gyroscopes, are therefore frequently combined with GPS in a Kalman Filter for improving accuracy (GPS/INS). In addition, a map-based pose correction is obtained by applying a *map matching* algorithm: Assuming that the vehicle is on the road, its estimated pose is corrected by projection onto the maximum likelihood (ML) estimate of the currently occupied road $r_{\hat{M}L}$ in the map (cf. Fig. 6.3). The map matching presented by (Hummel 2006) and (Pink and Hummel 2008) therefore exploits vehicle pose history, road network topology, and driving restrictions in a probabilistic framework. A lane-precise estimate is however not available.

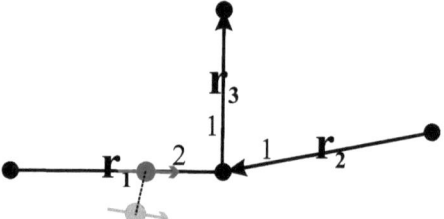

Figure 6.3: **Map Matching.** The red dots with arrows denote the vehicle position and orientation as delivered by GPS (light red), and the revised estimate yielded by map matching (saturated red).

A correct axiomatisation of the road estimate in RONNY is:

$$\mathcal{A}_{Localization} = \{$$
$$egolane \quad : \text{GPSInput} \sqcap \text{Lane} \quad ,$$
$$(egolane, r_{\hat{M}L}) : \text{alignedPartOf} \quad \} \; .$$

Because Lane is a ClosedWorldConcept, the individual named *egolane* cannot represent an additional lane on road $r_{\hat{M}L}$. Instead, the ABox now implies that

6.1. SENSOR SETUP

egolane must equal one of the introduced lanes of $r_{\hat{M}L}$. For example, if $r_{\hat{M}L} = r_1$:

$$\mathcal{KB} \models (egolane = l_{11} \vee egolane = l_{12}) \ .$$

Lane-precise pose estimation is thus turned into the standard reasoning task of data association (Sec. 4.3.4), and it is even performed collectively with classification.

Correct driver behaviour can additionally be assumed if desired. In case our vehicle is a car, and its estimated heading is towards the junction:

$$\mathcal{A}_{Localization, Driver} = \{$$
$$egolane : \textsf{MotorVehLane} \qquad ,$$
$$egolane : \exists \textsf{hasDrivingDirection.Entering} \ \} \ .$$

6.1.3 Stereo Camera

Computer Vision algorithms developed at the MRT comprise divider marking detection (Duchow 2006), lane detection (Duchow and Körtner 2007), path planning (Hummel et al. 2006), vehicle detection and tracking (Bachmann and Dang 2008), and initial work on arrow detection (Yang 2006). A classifier for divider types, however, is work in progress. For the present experiments, the divider class information was simulated to a reasonable extent (see next Subsection). In contrast to the map, no estimate concerning the total amount of objects is available (indeed, developing such an algorithm would be hard). The set of objects detected by video is therefore assumed *partial*, i. e. *not* of type ClosedWorldConcept.

Figure 6.4: **Vision-based Lane Detection.** The blue curves represent the detected dividers of the ego-lane (Fig. provided by C. Duchow).

Axiomatisation of Detections

Figure 6.4 exemplifies a typical detection result by the vision sensor. The detected individuals are introduced to RONNY as follows:

$$\mathcal{A}_{Camera, Detections} = \{$$
$$d_1 : \textsf{CameraInput} \sqcap \textsf{Divider} \ ,$$
$$d_2 : \textsf{CameraInput} \sqcap \textsf{Divider} \ \} \ .$$

The Camerainput classification states that the individual was provided by the camera sensor (accounting for Pattern SENSOR_SETUP). Further sensory input can be plugged in without change of the representation or reasoning architecture.

Axiomatisation of Classifications

Available classification information is formalised as:

$\mathcal{A}_{Camera, Classifications} = \{$
  d_1 : DividerMarking ⊓ Dashed ⊓ Single ⊓ 12cm ,
  d_2 : DividerMarking ⊓ Dashed ⊓ Single ⊓ 12cm $\}$.

Uncertainty can be axiomatised to a certain degree by using the ⊔ -constructor, e. g. as in Dashed ⊔ Solid, or by simply omitting specialisation into subclasses.

Axiomatisation of Spatial Relations

The introduction of new individuals requires knowing their qualitative absolute pose up to lane-precision (Sec. 6.1). In quantitative terms, this requires transforming 2D image coordinates to the earth-fixed UTM frame used by the map. Transforming from image to vehicle-fixed scene coordinates is done using our calibrated stereo camera setup, the online calibration of which is described in (Dang 2007) and (Dang and Hoffmann 2006). Transforming from vehicle-fixed to UTM coordinates is done using the vehicle pose estimator that was described in the previous Section.

Given the absolute pose, the spatial relations with respect to the introduced individuals of type ClosedWorldConcept can be computed on the Computer Vision side, and then be axiomatised as follows:

$\mathcal{A}_{Camera, spatialRelations} = \{$
  $(d_1, \overline{l_{i,j-1}})$: eastAlignedWith ,
  $(d_1, \overline{l_{ij}})$: westAlignedWith ,
  $(d_1, \overline{r_i})$: alignedPartOf   ,
  $(d_2, \overline{l_{ij}})$: eastAlignedWith ,
  $(d_2, \overline{l_{i,j+1}})$: westAlignedWith ,
  $(d_2, \overline{r_i})$: alignedPartOf
$\}$,

where l_{ij} denotes the lane in between the two dividers in Figure 6.4. All remaining relations are of type notAligned and are again added automatically by a rule. Stating the relations to ¬ClosedWorldConcept individuals is optional.

However, in reality a sufficiently accurate individual pose estimate will often be unavailable. In this case, it is alternatively possible to axiomatise the spatial relations only with respect to the introduced *egolane* individual. This is only feasible when omitting the instantiation of new individuals (recall that otherwise all relations with respect to ClosedWorldConcept individuals would have to be stated), and by using anonymous classes instead as follows:

$$\mathcal{A}_{Camera, spatial Relations} = \{$$
$$egolane : \exists eastAlignedWith.(DividerMarking$$
$$\sqcap Dashed \sqcap Single \sqcap 25cm) ,$$
$$egolane : \exists westAlignedWith.(DividerMarking$$
$$\sqcap Dashed \sqcap Single \sqcap 25cm)$$
$$\} .$$

Global pose estimation of the dividers thus becomes a matter of pose estimation of the *egolane*, as described in the previous Subsection, with the divider types providing additional constraints to the task.

6.2 Intersection Sample Set

RONNY's reasoning performance was evaluated on a sample set of 23 natural intersection scenes, thereof 19 urban intersections, 1 suburban intersection, and 3 freeway entrances/exits. Emphasis was put on choosing a large variety of intersections, especially including the most complex ones to find. For the urban intersections, a central traffic hub in the inner-city of Karlsruhe, Germany, the "Durlacher Tor", was picked. All intersections from a rectangular area around that hub, that were retrieved from the commercial digital map, were put into the sample set[1]. Figure 6.5 shows a map of the area from the local land surveying office. A high-resolution satellite image can be viewed with the Google Maps software at coordinates $(49.009093°, 8.417485°)$[2]. The suburban and the freeway intersections were included in the sample set to make sure that the model has not been too specially tailored to complex urban intersections.

For each intersection, the following steps were performed.

1. The GPS-based map matching algorithm was used for localisation of the vehicle on the road network. For the next intersection in driving direction,

---

[1] One exception was made here: At a few coordinates marked as intersections in the map, no change in road or lane structure occurs. These coordinates only serve to refine the geometrical slope of a road. They were not used as sample intersections, because this is not of interest here.

[2] URL: http://tinyurl.com/dx6dao

106   6. APPLICATION: DL-BASED INTERSECTION UNDERSTANDING

Figure 6.5: **Map for "Durlacher Tor" area in Karlsruhe, Germany, from landsurveying office.** Intersections retrieved from the digital map are highlighted in red. They constitute the experiments' sample set.

6.2. INTERSECTION SAMPLE SET

Figure 6.5: "Durlacher Tor" map continued.

the data retrieved from the digital map was mapped into a set of RONNY ABox assertions as described in Section 6.1.1.

The following steps were carried out at three different instants in time:
t_1 : entering the intersection (i. e. being on a Lane),
t_2 : on the actual junction (i. e. being on a LaneTransition),
t_3 : and leaving the intersection (i. e. being on a Lane again).

Data was added incrementally to the RONNY ABox at each time step.

2. The estimated vehicle pose was mapped into a set of RONNY ABox *egolane* assertions as described in Section 6.1.2. Recall that this estimate contains the vehicle's ego-road, but not its ego-lane. Furthermore, at time t_2, no pose information is available besides the fact "on junction". Correct driver behaviour was assumed in addition. Its axiomatisation is also described in Section 6.1.2.

3. With respect to vision, emphasis was put on simulating data realistically obtainable by a sensor. Two types of classifiers were assumed, and their data was mapped into a set of RONNY ABox assertions as described in Section 6.1.3:

   (a) Ego-lane divider type classifier: Provides the divider type for the left and right divider of the *egolane*, *if* the divider is clearly visible on the road (i. e. is not occluded by parking cars, for example), and *if* the vehicle is presently *not* on the junction (i. e. at t_1 and t_3), because the variety of markings present there is often misleading the vision algorithm.

   (b) Ego-lane divider geometry classifier: Provides the geometry of the *egolane* ∈ {GP1,GP2,GP3} on the junction (i. e. at t_2). This data could alternatively be obtained from vehicle trajectory classification.

The created ABox is referred to as $\mathcal{A}_i$, where i is the intersection number given in Figure 6.5. As an example, Figure 6.7 provides a pictorial representation of $\mathcal{A}_8$. It thus visualises the amount of available information when no background knowledge used. In DL terms, this is the information entailed by the KB under the *empty* TBox. Note that, without further assumptions, global map information cannot be associated with local positioning device and video information. The different sensors must therefore be displayed in separate subfigures. Note, too, that none of the tasks posed is solvable using the sensor data alone. Only few classifications become available when correct driver behaviour is assumed in addition (Fig. 6.7(f)). All visualisations in this chapter are based on the legend provided in Fig. 6.6.

6.2. INTERSECTION SAMPLE SET

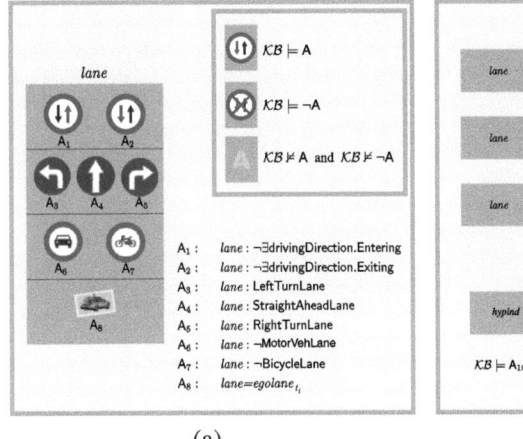
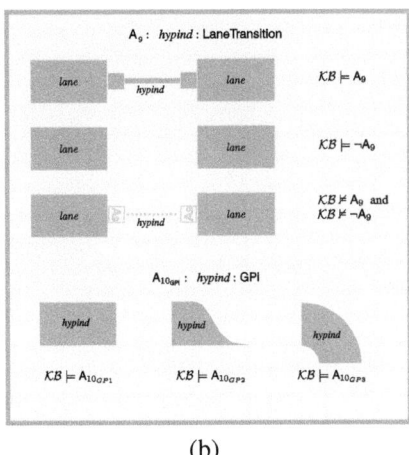

(a)   (b)

Figure 6.6: Figure Legend. *(a)* Each icon represents a concept or role assertion $A_i, i \in 1,..,8$, involving some Lane individual *lane*. The icon state visualises whether A_i, $\neg A_i$, or neither is entailed by the KB. *(b)* The three connectors visualise whether assertion A_9, $\neg A_9$, or neither is entailed by the KB for some ObjectHypothesis individual *hypind*. The three geometries visualise if one of $A_{10_{GPi}}, i \in \{1, 2, 3\}$, is entailed. If neither $A_{10_{GPi}}$ nor $\neg A_{10_{GPi}}$ is entailed for any i, only the line connector (cf. A_9) is displayed. $\neg A_{10_{GPi}}$ is not visualised.

In addition, a second, "ground truth" RONNY ABox $\mathcal{A}_{i,groundtruth}$ was created by hand for each intersection. It contained the correct assertions with respect to each of the tasks mentioned below. It was used as the reference against which the reasoning results for the ABoxes described above were compared, and for validating the intersection model through Experiment 1 (in Sec. 6.3.2).

110   6. APPLICATION: DL-BASED INTERSECTION UNDERSTANDING

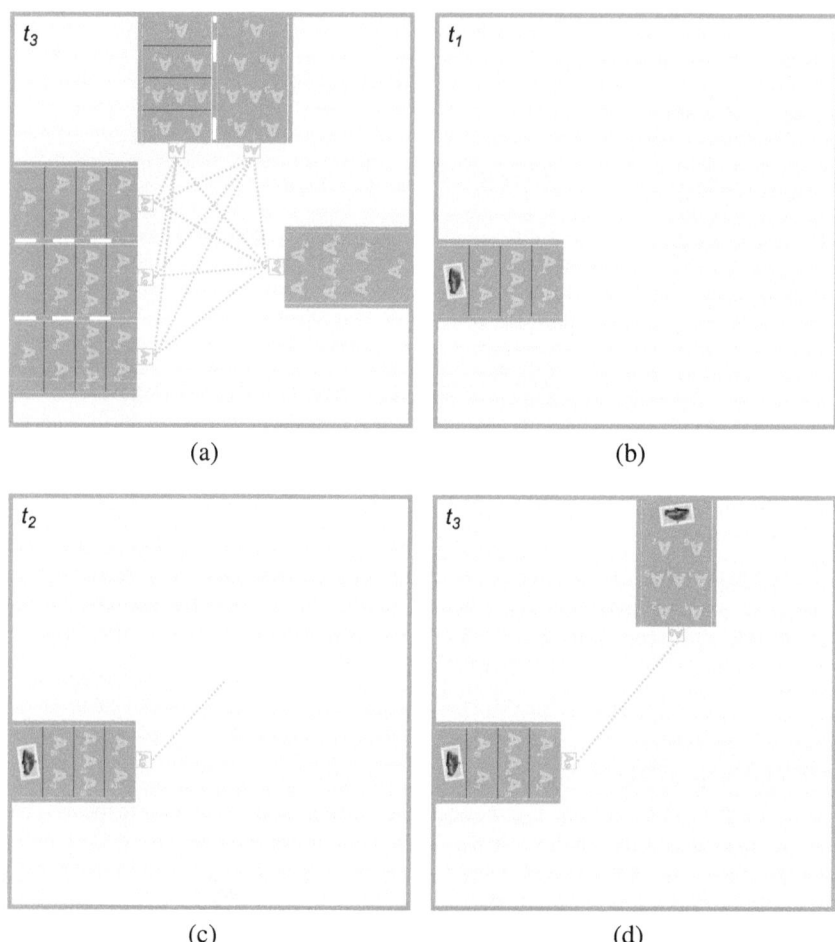

Figure 6.7: **Sensory Input during traversal of intersection 8.**   Pictorial representation of the amount of available information *before* reasoning, i. e when no background knowledge is applied.   *(a)* digital map data, *(b)-(d)* positioning device data at times t_1-t_3.   The map provides the number of roads aligned to the junction (three), their spatial arrangement (headingStraightAhead|Eastwards|Westwards), driving directions (OneWayEntering|OneWayExiting|¬OneWay) (not depictable in this representation), and number of lanes. No information about lane types or connectivity is contained. The position device provides the ego-road at t_1 and t_3, but not the ego-lane. (Continued on next page...)

6.2. INTERSECTION SAMPLE SET

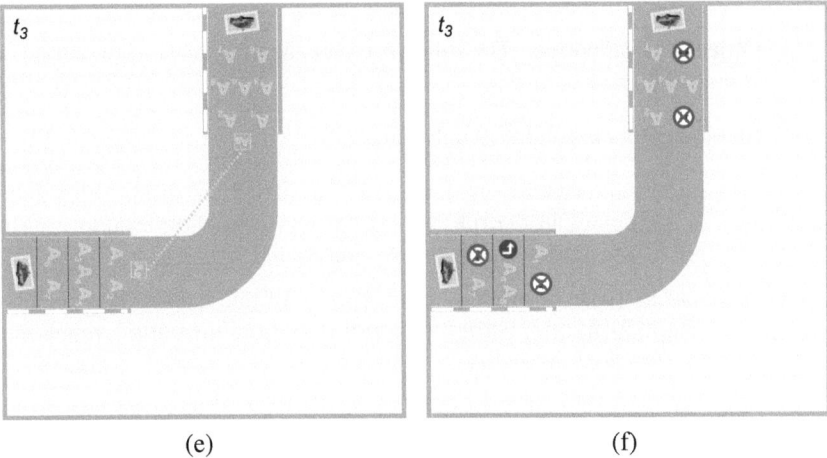

Figure 6.7: **Continued from previous page.** *(e)* positioning device and video data at t_3. The video sensor detected the eastern divider (Dashed ⊓ 12cm) of the ego-lane (with respect to the egocentric frame) at t_1 and t_3, respectively, and the geometric primitive (GP3) at t_2. However, it is unknown whether the depicted trajectory is actually a driveable path, as correct driver behaviour is not assumed. *(f)* positioning device and video data at t_3, when correct driver behaviour is assumed in addition: The *egolane* at t_1 lane allows for motorised vehicles, for entering the junction, and for doing a left turn. The *egolane* at t_3 allows for motorised vehicles and for exiting the junction (this has been visualised here although defining the meaning of these terms and deriving the corresponding deductions from the data would already require the RONNY TBox).

6.3 Experimental Results

The following experiments were carried out:

1. **Model Validation**: Is any of the assumptions in the RONNY TBox violated by the presented intersections? I. e., does the knowledge base become inconsistent for any ground truth ABox?

2. **Object Classification**: The following classification tasks were carried out at time instant t_3[3]:

    Classification of each Lane individual ...

    (a) into its allowed driving directions. The set of non-disjoint class labels is {∃drivingDirection.Entering, ∃drivingDirection.Exiting}. They are represented by assertions A_1 and A_2 in Figure 6.6.

    (b) into its types of turning lanes. The set of non-disjoint class labels is {RightTurnLane, StraightAheadLane, LeftTurnLane }, represented by assertions A_3 and A_5.

    (c) into its permitted types of traffic participants. The set of non-disjoint class labels is {MotorVehLane, BicycleLane }, represented by A_6 and A_7. The third relevant subclass, EmergencyLane, was left out from the classification task, because these lanes were not represented in the example intersections.

    Classification of each LaneTransition individual ...

    (d) into the disjoint subclasses representing qualitative geometry. The set of class labels is {GP1,GP2,GP3}, represented by assertion A_{10} in Figure 6.6.

3. **Object Detection**: Detection of driveable paths, i. e. LaneTransition individuals, between Lane pairs. This task is represented by assertion A_9 in Figure 6.6.

4. **Data Association**: Association of the *egolane*$_{t_i}$ with exactly one other Lane individual on the intersection. This task is represented by assertion A_8 in Figure 6.6.

---

[3] Initially experimental evaluation had been planned for time instants t_1, t_2 and t_3. This setup had to be abandoned because it turned out to be computationally not feasible. Evaluation at t_3 only has been chosen instead, since more information is then available compared to previous time instants.

6.3. EXPERIMENTAL RESULTS

Note that the class labels for each mentioned Lane classification task are *not disjoint*: A Lane can be driveable in both driving directions, it can allow for turning right and left at the same time, and it can allow for both cars and bicycles. Therefore each label can itself be seen as one *binary* classification task[4].

Experiments (2.)–(4.) are performed *collectively* by the reasoner for all individuals. Reasoning here initially terminated within acceptable time and without memory overflow for only 4 intersections. To reduce the complexity of the tasks, the assertions concerning vehicle position and correct driver behaviour were rewritten using anonymous classes:

Original formulation, exemplified for time t_1 (cf. Sec. 6.1.2):

$$\mathcal{A}_{Localization} = \{$$
$$egolane_{t_1} \quad : \text{GPSInput} \sqcap \text{Lane} \quad ,$$
$$(egolane_{t_1}, r_{\hat{ML}}) : \text{alignedPartOf} \quad ,$$
$$egolane_{t_1} \quad : \text{MotorVehLane} \quad ,$$
$$egolane_{t_1} \quad : \exists \text{hasDrivingDirection.Entering} \} .$$

Updated formulation:

$$\mathcal{A}_{Localization} = \{$$
$$r_{\hat{ML}} : \exists \text{alignedWithPart}.$$
$$\quad (\text{MotorVehLane} \sqcap \exists \text{hasDrivingDirection.Entering}) \} .$$

Both formulations express identical information, and in particular the vehicle's ego lane in the road remains unspecified in both cases. The latter assertions, however, prevent the introduction of three individuals, $egolane_{t_1}$, $egolane_{t_2}$ and $egolane_{t_3}$, and data association reasoning for them. The benefit is reduced complexity of reasoning, the cost is that Experiment 4 cannot be performed without these individuals. With this modification, reasoning terminated for 10 out of 23 intersection ABoxes.

The next section qualitatively analyses the collective reasoning result for one intersection example. The four subsequent sections describe the quantitative results with respect to the sample set of 23 (Experiment (1.)) / 10 (Experiment (2.)–(4.)) intersections.

---

[4]The traffic signs in the first and third row of Fig. 6.6(a) visualise the 'false' label of these classification tasks.

6.3.1 Example

Figure 6.8 exemplarily shows the result of reasoning for intersection 8, on the basis of the sensor input depicted in Figures 6.7, and visualised on the basis of Figure legend 6.6. In DL terms, it visualises the knowledge deductively entailed by a KB that consists of the ABox $\mathcal{A}_8$ and the RONNY TBox.

Providing formal proofs for these entailments would be non-explanatory, since each typically results from a long chain of deductions using many assertions and axioms. Instead shortened prosaic explanations are given, together with references to some of the axioms involved. Note, however, that considerably more axioms and assertions than the ones mentioned are required for these deductions.

Classification into Driving Directions (A_1 and A_2)

The map tells that road *durlacher_allee_west* is OneWayEntering, and roads *durlacher_allee_ost* and *bertholdstraße* are OneWayExiting. Each of the six Lanes is trivially classifiable therefrom by simply propagating the road's label. (axioms 1-2 in $\mathcal{T}_{DrivingDirection}$ (Sec. 5.3.3), and axioms 1-3 in $\mathcal{T}_{Defineables}$ (Sec. 5.1.5).

Positive Classification into Turning Lane Types (A_3 to A_5)

Each lane must be reachable by at least one driveable path (axiom 2 in $\mathcal{T}_{Paths}$ (Sec. 5.3.5)). The OneWayExiting lane of *durlacher_allee_ost* can only be reached by a lane which allows for ∃drivingDirection.Entering (same axiom), which rules out *bertholdstraße*. From the three lanes of *durlacher_allee_west*, at least the eastmost lane (with respect to the egocentric road frame) must be a StraightAheadLane. This is because in right-handed traffic, RightTurnLanes are east of StraightAheadLanes which are east of LeftTurnLanes (all axioms in $\mathcal{T}_{RightHandedTraffic}$ (Sec. 5.3.1)), and because there is no RightTurnLane on this road since there is no other road in headingEastwards from it (map data).

The notion of a driveable path implies that no lane-change is required (axioms 4 to 6 in $\mathcal{T}_{Paths}$ (Sec. 5.3.5)) and therefore a LeftTurnLane has exactly one driveable path westwards. For this reason, and to satisfy the reachability axiom mentioned above for the remaining lanes, the other two lanes of *durlacher_allee_west* and the two lanes of *bertholdstraße* must connect pairwise.

6.3. EXPERIMENTAL RESULTS

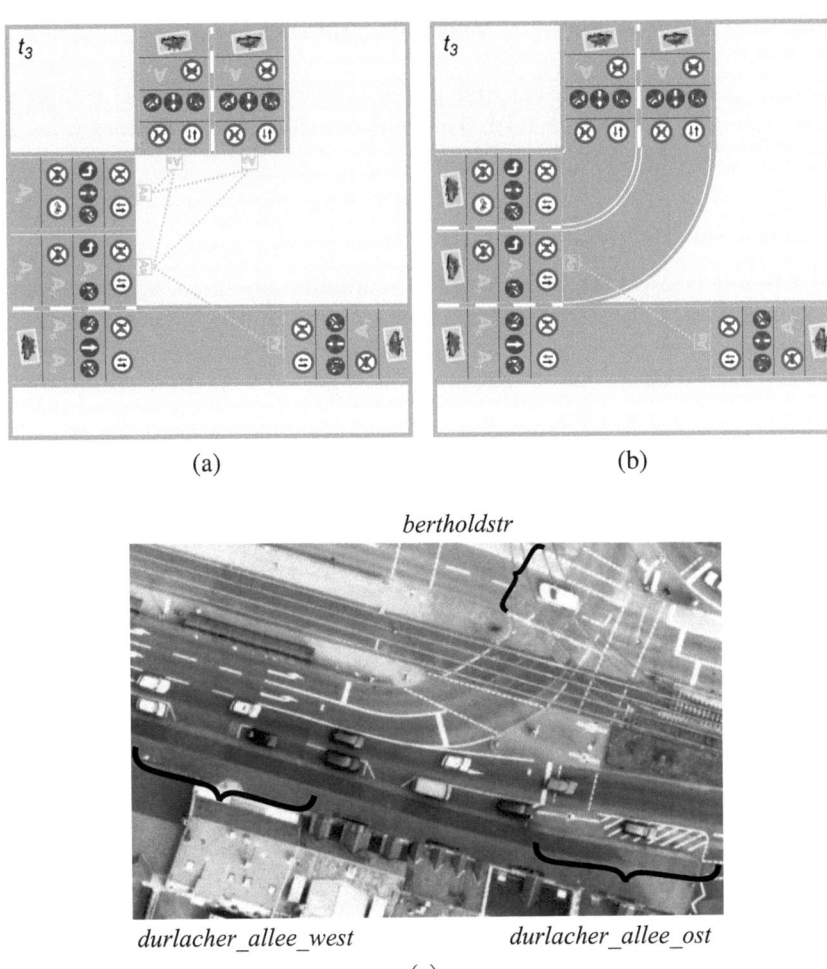

Figure 6.8: **Experiment Results for Intersection 8.** *(a)* Pictorial representation of the knowledge available *after* reasoning (compare to Figure 6.7). All three sensors and correct driver behaviour have been used as input (see Figs. 6.7(a) and 6.7(f)). *(b)* Knowledge available if at t_1 additionally the left divider of the ego-lane (**Dashed** ⊓ **12cm**) were detected by the vision sensor (Fig. 6.7(e)). The intersection is almost fully reconstructed with respect to the tasks, even though only a fraction of the information was contained explicitly in the sensors. *(c)* Satellite image of the intersection, together with the names of the **Road** instances. (Source: City of Karlsruhe, VLW geo data)

Negative Classification into Turning Lane Types (A_3 to A_5)

Only lanes which permit to enter the junction can be TurningLanes (defining axiom in $T_{Defineables}$ (Sec. 5.1.5)). This rules out all lanes of *durlacher_allee_ost* and *bertholdstraße* (from A_1 and A_2).

No lane of *durlacher_allee_west* can be a RightTurnLane because their is no road heading eastwards on that junction (map data).

Its leftmost lane cannot be a StraightAheadLane any more, because it has a LeftTurnLane as its east neighbour (axiom for right-handed traffic, see above). Its rightmost lane cannot be a LeftTurnLane any more, because all driveable paths to the eastwards road are "taken" already by its other two lanes (from positive A_3).

The only uncertainty left concerns the StraightAheadLane label for its middle lane: It could allow for turning left, as well as for driving straight ahead, because StraightAheadLanes may merge into one lane (axiom 6 in T_{Paths} (Sec. 5.3.5)).

Classification into Admissible Traffic Participants (A_6 and A_7)

Each road must have at least one MotorVehLane (axioms 1-2 in $T_{LaneTypes}$ (Sec. 5.3.4)). If there is a BicycleLane present, it must be the eastmost lane of its TurningLane type (axioms 9-11 in $T_{LaneTypes}$ (Sec. 5.3.4)). This yields the depicted classifications for lanes on *durlacher_allee_west* and *bertholdstraße*.

The vehicle is on *bertholdstraße* at t_3 (positioning device data). Because of the detected Dashed ⊓ 12cm eastern divider of the ego-lane at t_3 (video data), there must be another lane to the east of it (axiom 1 in $T_{Dividers}$ (Sec. 5.3.2)). As there are only two lanes on that road (map data, closure of Lane concept (sec. 6.1)), the vehicle is on the western one. That lane is a MotorVehLane (assumption of correct driver behaviour).

Data Association of Ego-Lane (A_8)

The ego-lane at t_3 is the westmost lane of *bertholdstraße* (from A_6 and A_7). The ego-lane at t_1 must be one of the two LeftTurnLanes (positioning device data, assumption of correct driver behaviour). This fact can also be derived from the divider at t_1 (vision sensor), from which it follows that there is some neighbouring lane east of the ego-lane (axiom 1 in $T_{Dividers}$ (Sec. 5.3.2)). However, it is unknown which of the two lanes the vehicle is on.

Detection of Lane Transitions (A_9) and Classification into Geometric Primitives (A_{10})

The StraightAheadLane of *durlacher_allee_west* (A_4) has a driveable path to *durlacher_allee_ost* lane, because it is the only lane straightAhead of it (map data, closure of Lane concept (sec. 6.1)). That path must be of geometric shape GP1. GP3 is ruled out because it is a StraightAheadLane (axiom 3 in $T_{PathGeometry}$ (Sec. 5.3.6)), and a GP2 shaped lane-merging may only occur on junctions with less than three aligned roads (axioms 5-6 in $T_{PathGeometry}$ (Sec. 5.3.6)).

Although the other two lanes of *durlacher_allee_west* have a left turning path (from A_3, and definition of LeftTurnLane in $T_{Definables}$ (Sec. 5.1.5)), for neither it is known to which *bertholdstraße* lane it leads. This is because the fact that lane transitions of the same TurningLane type may not cross cannot be axiomatised (cf. Sec. 5.3.5).

Conclusions

Several conclusions can be drawn from this brief analysis of the experimental outcome for ABox A_8: First, the representation in a joint formal framework makes it possible to fuse information from different sensors, such as the vision sensor and the map, even though the vehicle's ego-lane is not known and therefore precise data registration is not possible. Second, this fusion is possible despite the very diverse nature of the sensor data involved, ranging from high-level concepts describing functionality, like OneWayRoad, to mid-level concepts describing geometry, like 12cm or GP1. Third, joint reasoning yields a synergy effect: Considerably more conclusions can be drawn in total through joint reasoning, than if just adding up the information given by each sensor in isolation (compare Figures 6.7(a) and 6.7(f) with Figure 6.8(a)).

It is hard to demonstrate the benefits of a formal knowledge representation on an isolated example, because this provokes a response like "I could have coded that much simpler with *if-then* rules in my source code". Its benefits can instead only be demonstrated by showing their validity on a large and diverse sample set (for which the number of required *if-then* rules would combinatorially explode, and would most likely yield erroneous results), and by proving easy adaptability to different setups (such as other countries, other application areas, etc.). The next four sections provide quantitative results on the sample set of 23 intersections.

6.3.2 Model Validation

The first experiment is performed to test the validity of the model assumptions. This is done by checking consistency of each ground truth ABox $\mathcal{A}_{i,groundtruth}, i \in 1,..23$ with respect to the RONNY TBox. If an intersection ABox violates only one of the assumptions made in the TBox, it becomes inconsistent. This indicates that one or several assumptions in RONNY are too restrictive. In this case, the responsible axioms can be removed or modified. If no intersections are inconsistent, as a very diverse intersection sample set was chosen, it substantiates the claim that the hypothesis space spanned by the qualitative model RONNY comprises – at least – a very large subset out of the set of actually existent intersections in Germany.

Out of the 23 sampled intersections, 21 were classified consistent. The intersections with number 2 and 9 were inconsistent. In both cases, the inconsistency was due to the same cause: A lane designated for bicycles led to a separate bike path outside of the road network. These lanes are highlighted in Figure 6.9. They violated axiom 2 in $\mathcal{T}_{Paths}$ (Sec. 5.3.5), which states

> // No isolated lanes: A lane that connects to a junction
> // has some driveable path.
> Lane ⊓ ∃IonAligned.Junction ⊑ ∃IonAligned.LaneTransition   .

According to the scene geometry model (Sec. 5.2), LaneTransitions connect to exactly 2 Lanes, one on each end. As the complete set of Lanes is provided by the map, the Lane concept has been axiomatised as a *closed* concept (Sec. 6.1), which implies that no further lane must exist for that junction. However, the map only contains lanes that are part of the *road* network, but not separate bike paths. This causes the inconsistency.

RONNY must therefore be modified to account for the fact, that only lanes designated for *cars* require a driveable path to another lane on the *road* network. This is achieved by a small modification of the axiom:

> // No isolated lanes: A **motor vehicle** lane that connects to a junction
> // has some driveable path.
> **MotorVeh**Lane⊓ ∃IonAligned.Junction ⊑ ∃IonAligned.LaneTransition

With the modification, all 23 intersections classified consistent.

6.3. EXPERIMENTAL RESULTS

(a)   (b)

Figure 6.9: **Intersections 9 (left) and 2 (right) classified inconsistent.** The BicyclesOnlyLane which left the road network and therefore caused the inconsistency, is marked by a black arrow. (Source: City of Karlsruhe, VLW geo data)

6.3.3 Object Classification

The second Experiment assesses classification reasoning. Seven binary classification tasks were performed for all Lane individuals on each intersection. They are depicted in Fig. 6.6 as assertions $A_1 - A_7$. One ternary classification, $A_{GP_i}, i \in 1, 2, 3$, was performed for LaneTransitions.

Table 6.1 quantifies the results of each classification task for the 10 ABoxes for which reasoning terminated. All results are given in the form of a confusion table (see right Figure).

		Classification result		?
Ground	truth	#TP	#FP	#?P
		#FN	#TN	#?N

Diagonal entries denote the number of correct classifications of the presented positive (#TP, "true positive") and negative (#TN, "true negative") samples. Any number greater than zero on these entries represents a gain of information compared to a system that does not use RONNY. Anti-diagonal entries (#FP and #FN) denote misclassifications. As only deductive reasoning is performed, the system will only deduce an individual's class if its membership can be proven. A misclassification, just like an ABox inconsistency, therefore indicates either a TBox modelling error, or erroneous sensor data. #?P and #?N denote the number of unclassifiable samples. Obviously, each row sums to the total number of presented positive/negative samples.

The driving direction was classified correctly for all lanes. As this task is trivially

6. APPLICATION: DL-BASED INTERSECTION UNDERSTANDING

Table 6.1: Results for Object Classification. Refer to the legend in Fig. 6.6 and the text for explanation.

A_1 : $lane$: $\neg\exists drivingDirection.Entering$

	⊙	⊗	?
⊙	3 (21)	0	0
⊗	0	5 (21)	0

A_2 : $lane$: $\neg\exists drivingDirection.Exiting$

	⊙	⊗	?
⊙	3 (19)	0	0
⊗	0	5 (23)	0

A_3 : $lane$: LeftTurnLane

	↰	⊗	?
↰	3	0	0
⊗	0	36	3

A_4 : $lane$: StraightAheadLane

	↑	⊗	?
↑	12	0	2
⊗	0	25	3

A_5 : $lane$: RightTurnLane

	↱	⊗	?
↱	5	0	1
⊗	0	34	2

A_6 : $lane$: $\neg$MotorVehLane

	⊖	⊗	?
⊖	0	0	0
⊗	0	35	7

6.3. EXPERIMENTAL RESULTS

(Table 6.1 continued)

A_7 : *lane* : ¬BicycleLane

	⊙	⊗	?
⊙	9	0	22
⊗	0	0	11

$A_{10_{GPi}}$: *hypind* : GPi

	GP1	GP2	GP3	?
GP1	4	0	0	13
GP2	0	0	0	2
GP3	0	0	7	1

solvable by two *if-then*-rules for those cases, in which only OneWay roads are involved (the road class label just has to be propagated to the lanes' level), only the non-trivial cases have been used, that is those, where ¬OneWay roads are involved. The complete number is given in brackets behind. The task exhibited zero unclassifiable samples. Likewise, for almost all lanes the correct TurningLane type could be derived. This means that the permitted driving directions and turning lane types of almost all lanes of an intersection can be deduced without actual sensor data about most of them.

35 out of the 42 lanes were correctly classified as MotorVehLane. The sample set did not contain any ¬MotorVehLanes. It turned out to be hard to distinguish whether a MotorVehLane additionally allows for bicycles or not: Only 9 out of 42 lanes were classifiable into BicycleLane/¬BicycleLane. Closer observation yielded that RONNY does not make any restricting assumptions about bicycle lanes in urban areas. Most likely, hardly any hard constraints do actually apply there. Finally, the geometry of 11 out of 26 lane transitions could be deduced.

Zero misclassifications were observed for all classification tasks, providing additional indication that RONNY's domain model is able to represent a large variety of intersections.

6.3.4 Object Detection

Experiment 3 evaluates the detection rate on the task of detecting driveable paths, i. e. LaneTransition individuals, between each pair of Lanes on a junction. The existence of such a lane transition can either be Verified, making the hypothesised individual *hypind* an actual instance of a LaneTransition, or Falsified. If there is not enough information to perform the detection task, the individual will remain unclassified in that respect. The following Table quantifies the detection result.

Table 6.2: Results for Object Detection. Refer to the legend in Fig. 6.6 and the text for explanation.

A_9 : *hypind* : LaneTransition

	✓		?
✓	12	0	15
	0	9	17

Using the RONNY TBox, the existence of almost half of the actually present driveable paths, and of more than one third of the non-driveable paths could be proven. This is already a considerable gain in information. A limiting factor here, however, is the fact, that the $\mathcal{SHIQ}$ DL does not support role chains. It can therefore not be axiomatised that transitions from lanes of identical turning lane type must not cross (cf. Sec. 5.3.5), and rules provide only weak remedy here.

6.3.5 Data Association

Experiment 4 assesses the performance of data association. The object to be associated is the vehicle's ego-lane, and it can be associated with any of the lanes on the junction. In engineering terms, this task amounts to estimating the egopose of the experimental vehicle with lane precision. The task is posed for time instants t_1 (entering the junction) and t_3 (leaving the junction). In DL terms, association corresponds to unifying two individuals, i. e. $egolane_{t_k} = lane_i$ or to deducing their semantic inequality, i. e. $egolane_{t_k} \neq lane_i$, under the constraint the *exactly one* equality holds.

As explained at the beginning of this Section (Sec. 6.3), including this task in the collective reasoning leads to algorithm termination without a memory overflow for only 4 ABoxes. This results in the large number of results labelled with "?". For

Table 6.3: **Results for Data Association.** Refer to the legend in Fig. 6.6 and the text for explanation.

A_8 : *lane = egolane*

	🚗	🌳	?
🚗	8	0	12
🌳	0	5	59

the 4 terminating ABoxes, however, the vehicle's ego lane was correctly deduced at both time steps.

Given the amount of available sensor data, this task is not solvable without domain knowledge and a joint reasoning framework. The non-zero entries on the main diagonal of Table 6.3(a) therefore quantitatively demonstrate that DL-reasoning offers problem solving capacities that go *beyond* the possibilities of purely geometric Computer Vision algorithms.

6.4 Summary

It was demonstrated that deductive DL reasoning services are capable of performing the classic Computer Vision tasks of object detection, classification, and data association. It was shown that it serves as a beneficial supplement on top of an existing mid-level Computer Vision system, producing a significant set of additional results, but zero false positive and false negative results. The additional results were obtained from the constraints applied from background knowledge, and from the synergy effect achieved by joint evaluation of sensor data. Joint evaluation was possible even although a precise data registration between the vision sensor and the map was not available, and even though the description of the input data differed widely with respect to types and abstraction layers used.

Computational limits, however, allowed evaluation of only 10 out of 23 sample ABoxes, and when data association was included, only 4 out of 23 ABoxes could be evaluated.

The explicit and modular representation allowed to pinpoint modelling flaws, such as the one leading to the initial two ABox inconsistencies (Section 6.3.2), and to correct them at minimal expense, that is without requiring to update any other part of the representation.

The RONNY KB proved sufficiently general to represent a large subset of the intersections present in Germany. It is as well restrictive enough to produce a substantial amount of conclusions under realistic sensor data. RONNY was able to cope with incomplete as well as with locally complete sensor data, and with a redundant sensor setting.

7 Conclusion

7.1 Summary

The task of Scene Understanding requires a suitable representation and reasoning framework. No classical framework has so far proven the silver bullet for flexible understanding of natural scenes, and the required properties of such a formalism are not yet clear. Fortunately, the last decade witnessed the development of some promising formal languages, one of which is the Description Logic fragment of First Order Logic. The present thesis investigated the suitability of Description Logic as a representation and reasoning formalism for Scene Understanding. Complex road intersections were selected as the application domain, the expressive Description Logic $\mathcal{SHIQ}$ and the optimised RACERPRO reasoner as the reference framework.

An extensive literature survey concluded that logic-enhanced systems have not yet proven superior over state-of-the-art quantitative Computer Vision algorithms. It was argued, that some of the hoped-for advantages of logic –modularity, readability, semantic unambiguity, and thus reusability– can only become quantifiable when reasoning with a realistically large body of scene knowledge (otherwise a propositional language or even if-then rules in the source code would suffice). In analogy to object-oriented software engineering, engineering of such a knowledge base requires reusable KB modules, coding design patterns, and literature on KB engineering, for the Scene Understanding domain.

As a step in that direction, the present contribution elaborated on a principled translation of Computer Vision characteristics into the DL framework. Design patterns, intended for reuse, were proposed for some of these translations. It was argued that some crucial Computer Vision characteristics, such as incompleteness of sensor data, particularly of the number of detected objects, already map to DL's inherent representational paradigms. It was however also stated, that Computer Vision additionally requires the ability to express local completeness of information, which is not axiomatisable in DL. Therefore a pattern was provided which approximates the required closure axioms. In a next step, several typical sensor setups –partial/locally complete data in a redundant/complementary setup– were mapped into DL axioms. Addressing representation of geometry, a hypothesis space for qualitative scene geometries was proposed, along with a graphical UML-like specification language and a design pattern for its translation into DL. It was shown that several classic Computer Vision problems –object detection, object classification, and data association– can be solved by classic DL reasoning services, and corresponding design patterns were provided for each.

An extensive case study in the domain of road networks has been conducted. The road network ontology RONNY was introduced, a $\mathcal{SHIQ}$ TBox which models the qualitative geometry and building regulations of road intersections for the purpose of Scene Understanding. It makes extensive use of the design patterns proposed before. The set of ABoxes that is consistent with the RONNY TBox corresponds to the hypothesis space of admissible intersections that is set up by the RONNY model. An ABox consists of arbitrary intersection sensor data that is formulated in the RONNY vocabulary.

A quantitative evaluation of DL reasoning capabilities with respect to Intersection Understanding and of the applicability of RONNY's domain model was performed. It was based on a sample set of 23 diverse and complex intersections from urban and non-urban roads in Germany. Three sensors, a digital map, a global positioning device and a realistic simulation of vision-based object detectors, were used as data input. For each intersection, DL reasoning was applied to a couple of Scene Understanding tasks, namely: Which driving directions does each lane permit (classification task) ? Which traffic participants (bicycles, cars) are allowed on each lane (classification task)? Between which lane pairs do driveable paths exist (detection task)? Which of the map's lanes is equivalent to the ego-lane (data association task)?

RONNY's intersection model has been shown to be expressive, as all intersections in the sample set are contained in its hypothesis space. Yet it has been shown to be restrictive enough to yield a substantial amount of additional correct conclusions about the intersection scene, particularly in areas where no sensor data is available.

7.2 Evaluation: Description Logic for Scene Understanding

Based on the experiences gathered during the case study, the following paragraph evaluates the overall suitability of the Description Logic formalism to Scene Understanding.

7.2. EVALUATION: DESCRIPTION LOGIC FOR SCENE UNDERSTANDING

Reasoning Services

+ Collective Reasoning DL reasoning is performed jointly for all tasks posed and for all individuals. This provides for a considerable synergy effect during reasoning: More conclusions can be drawn through joint reasoning than by adding up the conclusions drawn from each sensor in isolation.

+ Deductive Reasoning Several classic Computer Vision reasoning tasks have been shown to be readily solvable by classic deductive DL reasoning. In addition, deduction will not force any result under insufficient information (zero false positives or true negatives provided that the domain model is correct).

− Non-monotonic Reasoning Non-monotonic inferences are not supported by classic deductive DL reasoning. This means that a once drawn conclusion can never be invalidated in the future. According to a modern understanding of vision, however, hypotheses are generated under highly incomplete evidence (e. g. (Gregory 1997)), which implies that the arrival of new information will oftentimes trigger the revision of previous beliefs. Promising extensions of DL to support this type of reasoning are discussed in the Outlook.

Knowledge Representation

+ First-order Language The first-order representation proved very beneficial in representing "generic hypothesis spaces", that is those, whose number and type of free parameters depends on the particular problem instance. As an example, the number of classification tasks to be solved varied between 21 (for intersection $\mathcal{A}_1$), and 105 (for intersection $\mathcal{A}_9$). The problem representation thereby also changed structure considerably. A propositional language would require tailoring the representation to each such instance. A sample set as diverse as the one considered here would not be feasible in a propositional language.

+ KR Paradigms The Open World Assumption and the Open Domain Assumption, two representational paradigms underlying DL, are required for a representation language for Scene Understanding (see Section 4.3).

+ Sensor Data Integration The formal framework makes it possible to fuse qualitative data from different sensing devices. This is possible even though this data internally differs widely with respect to type and abstraction layer of the descriptions of instances (e. g. an UrbanRoad vs. a 12cm divider width, ...), and of the relations that hold among them (e. g. geometric vs. functional, ...). Data fusion is possible even if precise data registration is not available (e. g. between a map and a vision sensor).

– **Spatial Calculi** $\mathcal{SHIQ}$ does not offer role-forming constructors. For the axiomatisation of spatial calculi, the lacking expressiveness of role disjointness, and of role coverage by other roles, is particularly problematic, as the JEPD property is not axiomatisable then. Although the present thesis proposed a workable approximation through closures, this property makes $\mathcal{SHIQ}$ not an ideal candidate for spatial reasoning, a crucial component of a Scene Understanding system.

– **No feature/role chains** As DL is a two-variable fragment of FOL, and as $\mathcal{SHIQ}$ does not offer feature/role chains, relations between three or more individuals cannot be expressed in that formalism. Trigger rules cannot be used as a remedy in every case. This can considerably limit the number of drawable inferences for complex relational domains.

Knowledge Engineering

+ Modularity The representation proved explicit and modular enough to pinpoint modelling flaws, such as the one leading to the initial two ABox inconsistencies (Section 6.3.2), and to correct them at minimal expense, that is without requiring to update any other part of the representation.

+ Developer and User Community The Semantic Web initiative has fostered a lively mutual exchange between developer and user community, making it possible that perceived shortcomings of the language and the implementations are rapidly tackled by the developers. Such an interaction is crucial since a KR formalism will require continuous adjustment to meet current and future requirements of Scene Understanding.

+/– Readability The representation is modular, explicit, and follows an object-oriented paradigm. This makes the KB well readable. However, the lacking language expressiveness mentioned above has a negative impact here. As for some roles, role semantics is not properly axiomatisable (such as roles that are defined on the basis of other roles (like the Neighbourhood relations, which are based on the Alignedness relations (Sec. 5)), counterintuitive reasoning behaviour is sometimes observed, which in turn requires more extensive KB documentation. It furthermore forces the knowledge engineer to resort to trigger rules and to programming language workarounds, which also decrease readability and modularity.

– **Computational Performance and Maturity of Implementations** A RONNY KB, that is a $\mathcal{SHIQ}$ KB containing about 50 concepts, 30 roles, and about 600 ABox assertions for a medium complex intersection, is at the computational limit of what is achievable with current DL reasoning technology. Reasoning about such an intersection takes about one hour. During TBox development, it can take several hours to find out (via memory overflow) that a coded axiom increases KB complexity too far. Given that RACERPRO is likely to be the most highly optimised ABox reasoner on the market, the integration with other KBs concerning vehicles or legal traffic rules –which might yield an impressive Scene Understanding system– is outside the scope of current reasoners. In addition, the technology is still evolving. In the course of the above case study, a considerable number of bugs were reported (and corrected by the developers!). These factors slow down KB development by a large amount.

In summary, the $\mathcal{SHIQ}$ DL and the RACERPRO implementation have proven a suitable representation and reasoning framework for Scene Understanding, naturally meeting many characteristics of Scene Understanding per se, and allowing for sound knowledge engineering. However, each of the mentioned downsides must be addressed before full-fledged DL-based Scene Understanding systems can be envisaged.

7.3 Outlook

7.3.1 Hypothesis Formation: Model Construction

A combination of deductive and hypothetical reasoning seems adequate for general Scene Interpretation. This view is also taken by (Schröder 1999), (Poole 1989) and (Neumann and Möller 2006). This requires extending classic DL reasoning services to support non-monotonic reasoning. Such *hypothetico-deductive* reasoning can enable a very desirable reasoning task for Scene Understanding, so-called *model construction*. It denotes the automatic construction of the set of all scene hypotheses given the sensor data and the background knowledge. In logical terms, this amounts to computing the set of all logical models of the KB. The following paragraphs sketch three extensions of deductive DL reasoning, that would enable model construction.

Modification of a Tableau Calculus

In principle, the development of a model construction algorithm can build on the research on *Tableau Calculi* which are used for satisfiability testing of TBoxes and consistency testing of ABoxes (cf. e. g. (Baader et al. 2003)). They apply a set of so-called consistency-preserving completion rules to the original ABox. The presence of ∃ and ⊔ symbols in the TBox triggers so-called non-deterministic rules which split the ABox in a depth-first-search way. The process stops when no more rules can be applied or when an obvious contradiction occurs. In the first case the generated model satisfies all TBox and all ABox axioms. The latter proves that the knowledge base is inconsistent. Tableau calculi thus create a model of the KB as a proof for its satisfiability.

However, tableau calculi are not straightforwardly applicable to Scene Interpretation, as they do not output the model but a mere yes/no answer, as they are highly optimised and therefore produce rather "canonical models", and as they stop after having found one model, preferring simpler ones. The implementation of a special-tailored calculus would be required instead. The following two alternatives are therefore more promising.

Abduction

In a DL context, abduction refers to the task of *explaining* a set of ABox assertions Γ by a given DL knowledge base $\mathcal{KB}$ and a further set of assertions, the *hypothesis* or *theory* Δ. After adding the hypothesis to the set of axioms, the observations follow as a logical consequence:

$$\mathcal{KB} \sqcup \Delta \models \Gamma$$

Using abduction and deduction in concert, a Scene Interpretation system can be realised: First, the most promising hypotheses are formed that might explain the sensor data using abduction. Second, the most promising hypothesis according to some preference measure is added to $\mathcal{KB}$. Third, the consequences of the hypothesis are computed using deduction. Finally, based on the new knowledge a new selective active sensory measurement is carried out, leading back to step one (Shanahan 2005). (Möller and Neumann 2008) have recently presented the first account of abductive-deductive reasoning in DL. Preparing the developed knowledge base to allow for abduction, and then using the recently published prototypical RACERPRO implementation of abduction, is a promising step towards a full-fledged DL-based Scene Understanding architecture.

Answer Set Programming

Answer Set Programming (ASP) emerged in the late 1990s as a powerful non-monotonic logic-programming paradigm (cf. Chapter 1). Recently, research efforts are made to combine ASP with DL, see e. g. the *DL programs* introduced by (Schindlauer 2006). With comparatively little effort, it might be possible to port the DLKB developed in this contribution to an ASP solver, which then computes the set of Scene Interpretation hypotheses as its answer sets. To the best of the author's knowledge, ASP has not been used for Scene Interpretation yet.

7.3.2 Probabilistic Logic Learning

Uncertain knowledge cannot be represented within the classic logic formalism. Although research efforts are under way to combine DL with probability theory, no robust implementation seems in sight for the near future. However, by the time of finishing this thesis, a new field called *Probabilistic Logic Learning* had just formed ((Getoor and Taskar 2007), and cf. also Chapter 1). This field unifies research on logic, probability theory, and machine learning under a common algorithmic roof. Implementations are right now in an early beta stadium. (Bachmann and Lulcheva 2009) have demonstrated the applicability of these formalisms in a Computer Vision context. It would be insightful to conduct the following experiment: First, port RONNY and the sample intersection ABoxes to FOL. Such a logically equivalent FOL formulation is easily constructible, as DL is a fragment of FOL and as e. g. (Baader et al. 2003) provides a unique mapping. Second, add more, soft formulas about typical intersection structures. Third, use an available implementation like ALCHEMY to learn weights for these formulas from the sample intersections, the weights corresponding to the truthfulness of these formulas. And finally, use that implementation to compute the marginal probabilities of any of the query assertions described in Chapter 6, given some example intersection as the evidence. Ideally, this will yield the conditional probability of the query assertion given the evidence, the hard RONNY formulas, and the soft formulas, for each individual. This approach might be able to combine sound knowledge engineering, as enabled by the mature and tool-supported DL framework, with a probabilistic learning framework.

Bibliography

M. Arens and H.-H. Nagel. Representation of behavioral knowledge for planning and plan-recognition in a cognitive vision system. In *KI '02: Proceedings of the 25th Annual German Conference on AI*, pages 268–282, London, UK, 2002. Springer-Verlag. ISBN 3-540-44185-9.

M. Arens and H.-H. Nagel. Quantitative movement prediction based on qualitative knowledge about behavior. *KI - Künstliche Intelligenz 2/2005 (Schwerpunkt: Cognitive Vision)*, 2:5–11, 2005.

F. Baader, D. Calvanese, D. L. McGuinness, D. Nardi, and P. F. Patel-Schneider, editors. *The Description Logic Handbook: Theory, Implementation, and Applications*. Cambridge University Press, 2003.

A. Bachmann and T. Dang. Improving motion-based object detection by incorporating object-specific knowledge. *International Journal of Intelligent Information and Database Systems (IJIIDS), Special Issue on: Information Processing in Intelligent Vehicles and Road Applications*, 2(2):258–276, 2008.

A. Bachmann and I. Lulcheva. Bayesian scene segmentation incorporating motion constraints and category-specific information. In *International Conference on Computer Vision Theory and Applications*, pages 291–298, 2009.

D.H. Ballard and C.M. Brown. *Computer Vision*. Prentice Hall, 1982.

Y. Bar-Shalom. *Tracking and data association*. Academic Press Professional, Inc., San Diego, CA, USA, 1987. ISBN 0-120-79760-7.

C. Baral. *Knowledge Representation, Reasoning and Declarative Problem Solving*. Cambridge University Press, February 2003. ISBN 0521818028.

B. Bennett, D. R. Magee, A. G. Cohn, and D. C. Hogg. Enhanced tracking and recognition of moving objects by reasoning about spatio-temporal continuity. *Image and Vision Computing*, 26(1):67–81, 2008.

A. Borgida and L. Serafini. Distributed description logics: Assimilating information from peer sources. *J. Data Semantics*, 1:153–184, 2003.

R. J. Brachman and H. J. Levesque. The tractability of subsumption in frame-based description languages. In *AAAI*, pages 34–37, 1984.

F. Bremond, M. Thonnat, and M. Zuniga. Video understanding framework for automatic behavior recognition. *Behavior Research Methods*, 3(38):416–426, 2006.

D. Calvanese, G. De Giacomo, M. Lenzerini, D. Nardi, and R. Rosati. Information integration: Conceptual modeling and reasoning support. In *Proc. 6th Int. Conf. on Cooperative Information Systems (CoopIS)*, pages 280–291, 1998.

W. W. Cohen and H. Hirsh. Learning the classic description logic: Theoretical and experimental results. In *In Principles of Knowledge Representation and Reasoning: Proceedings of the Fourth International Conference (KR94*, pages 121–133. Morgan Kaufmann, 1994.

A. G. Cohn and J. Renz. Qualitative spatial representation and reasoning. In F. van Hermelen, V. Lifschitz, and B. Porter, editors, *Handbook of Knowledge Representation*, chapter 13. Elsevier, 2007.

A.G. Cohn, D.C. Hogg, B. Bennett, V. Devin, A. Galata, D.R. Magee, C. Needham, and P. Santos. Cognitive vision: Integrating symbolic qualitative representations with computer vision. In H. I. Christensen and H.-H. Nagel, editors, *Cognitive Vision Systems: Sampling the Spectrum of Approaches*, volume 3948 of *Lecture Notes in Computer Science*, pages 221–246. Springer Berlin / Heidelberg, 2006.

A. Colmerauer, H. Kanoui, R. Pasero, and P. Roussel. Un système de communication en francais. Technical report, Groupe de Recherche en Intelligence Artificielle, University II Aix-Marseille, 1972.

T. Dang. *Kontinuierliche Selbstkalibrierung von Stereokameras*. Dissertation, Universität Karlsruhe (TH), Karlsruhe, 2007. URL http://www.uvka.de/univerlag/volltexte/2007/232/. Schriftenreihe Institut für Mess- und Regelungstechnik, Universitätsverlag Karlsruhe, Nr. 008.

T. Dang and C. Hoffmann. Tracking camera parameters of an active stereo rig. In *28th Annual Symposium of the German Association for Pattern Recognition (DAGM 2006)*, Berlin, September 12-14 2006.

M. Davies. Knowledge (explicit and implicit): Philosophical aspects. In N. J. Smelser and P. B. Baltes, editors, *International Encyclopedia of the Social and Behavioral Sciences*, volume 12, pages 8126–8132. Elsevier Science Ltd. Amsterdam, 2001.

C. Duchow. A novel, signal model based approach to lane detection for use in intersection assistance. In *IEEE Intelligent Transportation Systems Conference*, 2006.

C. Duchow and B. Körtner. Aggregating lane markings into lanes for intersection assistance. In *Proc. IEEE Intelligent Vehicles Symposium*, pages 722–727, Istanbul, Turkey, June 2007.

O. Etzioni, K. Golden, and D. Weld. Tractable closed-world reasoning with updates. In *Proc. 4th Int. Conf. on Principles of Knowledge Representation and Reasoning*, pages 178–189, 1994.

A. Finzi, F. Pirri, M. Pirrone, M. Romano, and M. Vaccaro. Autonomous mobile manipulators managing perception and failures. In *AGENTS '01: Proceedings of the fifth international conference on Autonomous agents*, pages 196–203, NY, USA, 2001.

E. Gamma, R. Helm, Johnson R., and J. Vlissides. *Design Patterns: Elements of Reusable Object-Oriented Software*. Addison-Wesley, 1995.

M. Gelfond and V. Lifschitz. The stable model semantics for logic programming. In Robert A. Kowalski and Kenneth Bowen, editors, *Proceedings of the Fifth International Conference on Logic Programming*, pages 1070–1080, Cambridge, Massachusetts, 1988. The MIT Press.

L. Getoor and B. Taskar. *Introduction to Statistical Relational Learning (Adaptive Computation and Machine Learning)*. The MIT Press, August 2007.

R. L. Gregory. Knowledge in perception and illusion. *Philosophical Transactions of the Royal Society B (Biological Sciences)*, 352(1358):1121–1128, August 1997.

S. Grimm and P. Hitzler. Semantic matchmaking of web resources with local closed-world reasoning. *International Journal of e-Commerce*, 12(2):89–126, JAN 2008.

B. N. Grosof, I. Horrocks, R. Volz, and S. Decker. Description logic programs: combining logic programs with description logic. In *WWW '03: Proceedings of the 12th international conference on World Wide Web*, pages 48–57, NY, USA, 2003.

V. Haarslev and R. Möller. Racer: A core inference engine for the Semantic Web. In Y. Sure and O. Corcho, editors, *Proc. 2nd International Workshop on Evaluation of Ontology-based Tools (EON2003), located at the 2nd International Semantic Web Conference ISWC*, volume 87, pages 27–36, Florida, USA, 2003.

A. Hanson and E. Riseman. *Segmentation of Natural Scenes. Computer Vision System*. Academic Press, New York, 1978.

C. Hewitt. Planner: A language for proving theorems in robots. In *Proceedings of First IJCAI, CA*, pages 295–301. Morgan Kaufman, 1969.

I. Horrocks and P. F. Patel-Schneider. A proposal for an OWL rules language. In *In Proc. 13th ACM International World Wide Web Conference (WWW)*, 2004.

I. Horrocks and U. Sattler. A tableau decision procedure for SHOIQ. *Journal of Automated Reasoning*, 39(3):249–276, 2007.

L. Hotz and B. Neumann. Scene interpretation as a configuration task. *KI*, 19(3): 59–, 2005.

B. Hummel. *Dynamic and Mobile GIS: Investigating Changes in Space and Time*, chapter Map Matching for Vehicle Guidance. CRC Press, 2006.

B. Hummel, S. Kammel, T. Dang, C. Duchow, and C. Stiller. Vision-based path-planning in unstructured environments. In *Proceedings of the IEEE Intelligent Vehicles Symposium*, pages 176–181, 2006.

B. Hummel, Z. Yang, and C. Duchow. Kreuzungsverstehen – ein wissensbasierter Ansatz. *IT-Schwerpunktheft Fahrerassistenzsysteme*, 1:5–16, 2007.

S. Kammel, J. Ziegler, B. Pitzer, M. Werling, T. Gindele, D. Jagszent, J. Schröder, M. Thuy, M. Goebl, F. von Hundelshausen, O. Pink, C. Frese, and C. Stiller. Team annieway's autonomous system for the 2007 darpa urban challenge. *Journal of Field Robotics*, 25(9):615 – 639, September 2008.

T. Kanade. Artificial vision: Progress and non-progress. In *Talk at the Dartmouth Artificial Intelligence Conference: The Next 50 Years*, 2006.

V. Kastrinaki, M. Zervakis, and K. Kalaitzakis. A survey of video processing technqiues for traffic applications. *Image and Vision Computing*, 21:359–381, 2003.

A. Lattner. *Temporal Pattern Mining in Dynamic Environments*. PhD thesis, Universitaet Bremen, DISKI 309, Akademische Verlagsgesellschaft GmbH Berlin, 2007.

B. Leibe, A. Leonardis, and B. Schiele. Robust object detection with interleaved categorization and segmentation. *International Journal of Computer Vision, Special Issue on Learning for Recognition and Recognition for Learning*, 77 (1–3):259–289, 2008a.

B. Leibe, K. Schindler, N. Cornelis, and L. Van Gool. Coupled object detection and tracking from static cameras and moving vehicles. *IEEE Trans. Pattern Analysis and Machine Intelligence*, 30(10):1683–1698, 2008b.

D. G. Lowe. Distinctive image features from scale-invariant keypoints. *International Journal of Computer Vision*, 60(2):91–110, 2004.

D. Magee, C. J. Needham, P. Santos, A. G. Cohn, and D. C. Hogg. Autonomous learning for a cognitive agent using continuous models and inductive logic programming from audio-visual input. In *Proceedings of the AAAI Workshop on Anchoring Symbols to Sensor Data*, 2004.

T. Matsuyama. Expert systems for image processing: Knowledge-based composition of image analysis processes. *Computer Vision, Graphics, and Image Processing*, 48(1):22–49, October 1989.

T. Matsuyama and V. Hwang. Sigma: A framework for image understanding - integration of bottom-up and top-down analysis. In *IJCAI*, pages 908–915, 1985.

J. C. McCall and M. M. Trivedi. Video-based lane estimation and tracking for driver assistance: Survey, system, and evaluation. *IEEE Transactions on Intelligent Transportation Systems*, 7:1:20–37, 2006.

J. McCarthy and P. J. Hayes. Some philosophical problems from the standpoint of artificial intelligence. In B. Meltzer and D. Michie, editors, *Machine Intelligence 4*, pages 463–502. Edinburgh University Press, 1969. reprinted in McC90.

P. McCorduck. *Machines Who Think*. W.H. Freeman, San Franzisco, 1979.

M. Minsky. A framework for representing knowledge. In *The Psychology of Computer Vision*. Massachusetts Institute of Technology, Cambridge, MA, USA, 1975.

R. Möller. Expressive description logics: Foundations for practical applications, habilitation thesis. University of Hamburg, Computer Science Department, July 2001.

R. Möller and B. Neumann. Ontology-based reasoning techniques for multimedia interpretation and retrieval. In Y. Kompatsiaris P. Hobson, editor, *Semantic Multimedia and Ontologies : Theory and Applications*. Springer, 2008.

R. Möller, C. Schröder, and C. Lutz. Analyzing configuration systems with description logics: A case study. Technical report, University of Hamburg, Computer Science Department, 1996.

R. Möller and T. H. Näth. Implementing probabilistic description logics: An application to image interpretation. In Anthony G. Cohn, David C. Hogg, Ralf Möller, and Bernd Neumann, editors, *Logic and Probability for Scene Interpretation*, number 08091 in Dagstuhl Seminar Proceedings, Dagstuhl, Germany, 2008.

B. Motik, I. Horrocks, R. Rosati, and U. Sattler. Can OWL and logic programming live together happily ever after? In *Proc. International Semantic Web Conference*, pages 501–514, 2006.

S. Muggleton. Inductive logic programming. *New Generation Computing*, 8(4): 295–318, 1991.

B. Neumann. Bildverstehen – ein Überblick. In G. Görz, C.-R. Rollinger, and J. Schneeberger, editors, *Handbuch der künstlichen Intelligenz*, pages 815–838. Oldenburg Wissenschaftsverlag, 2003.

B. Neumann and R. Möller. On scene interpretation with description logics. In H. I. Christensen and H.-H. Nagel, editors, *Cognitive Vision Systems: Sampling the Spectrum of Approaches*, volume 3948 of *Lecture Notes in Computer Science*, pages 247–278. Springer Berlin / Heidelberg, 2006.

J. Pearl. *Probabilistic reasoning in intelligent systems: networks of plausible inference*. Morgan Kaufmann Publishers Inc., San Francisco, CA, USA, 1988.

O. Pink and B. Hummel. A statistical approach to map matching using road network geometry, topology and vehicular motion constraints. In *Proc. Intelligent Transportation Systems*, 2008.

F. Pirri and A. Finzi. An approach to perception in theory of actions: Part i. *Electron. Trans. Artif. Intell.*, 3(C):19–61, 1999.

D. Poole. Explanation and prediction: An architecture for default and abductive reasoning. *Computational Intelligence*, 5(2):97–110, 1989.

R. Provine, C. Schlenoff, S. Balakirsky, S. Smith, and M. Uschold. Ontology-based methods for enhancing autonomous vehicle path planning. *Robotics and Autonomous Systems*, 49(1-2):123–133, 2004.

M. R. Quillian. Word concepts: a theory and simulation of some basic semantic capabilities. *Behavioral Science*, 12(5):410–430, September 1967. ISSN 0005-7940.

D. A. Randell, Z. Cui, and A. Cohn. *A Spatial Logic Based on Regions and Connection*, pages 165–176. Morgan Kaufmann, San Mateo, California, 1992.

R. Rao and R. Jain. Knowledge representation and control in computer vision systems. *Vision/Robotics*, pages 64–79, 1988.

RASt. *Richtlinien für die Anlage von Stadtstraßen*. Forschungsgesellschaft für Straßen- und Verkehrswesen, 2007.

R. Reiter and A. K. Mackworth. A logical framework for depiction and image interpretation. *Artificial Intelligence*, 41(2):125–155, 1989. ISSN 0004-3702.

L. Roberts. Machine perception of three-dimensional solids. In J. Tippett et al., editor, *Optical and Electro-optical Information Processing*, pages 159–197. MIT Press, 1965.

R. Rosati. Autoepistemic description logics. *AI Commun.*, 11(3-4):219–221, 1998.

S. Russell and P. Norvig. *Artificial Intelligence: A Modern Approach*. Prentice Hall, 1995.

C. Saathoff and S. Staab. Exploiting spatial context in image region labelling using fuzzy constraint reasoning. In *Proc. of WIAMIS 2008*, 2008.

R. Schindlauer. *Answer-Set Programming for the Semantic Web*. PhD thesis, Wien, 2006.

M. Schmidt-Schauß. Subsumption in KL-ONE is undecidable. In *Proc. of 1st Conf. on Knowledge Representation and Reasoning*, pages 421–431, 1989.

C. Schröder. *Bildinterpretation durch Modellkonstruktion: Eine Theorie zur rechnergestützten Analyse von Bildern*. DISKI 196, Infix, 1999.

O. G. Selfridge. Pattern recognition and modern computers. In *Western Joint Computer Conference*, pages 91–93, 1955.

M. Shah. Guest introduction: The changing shape of computer vision in the 21st century. *International Journal of Computer Vision*, 50(2):103–110, 2004.

M. Shanahan. Perception as abduction: Turning sensor data into meaningful representation. *Cognitive Science*, 29(1):103–134, 2005.

E. Sirin, B. Parsia, B. Grau, A. Kalyanpur, and Y. Katz. Pellet: A practical owl-dl reasoner. *Web Semantics: Science, Services and Agents on the World Wide Web*, 5(2):51–53, June 2007.

B. Taskar, P. Abbeel, and D. Koller. Discriminative probabilistic models for relational data. In *Proc. Eighteenth Conference on Uncertainty in Artificial Intelligence (UAI)*, Edmonton, Canada, 2002.

B. Taskar, M.-F. Wong, P. Abbeel, and D. Koller. Link prediction in relational data. In Sebastian Thrun, Lawrence Saul, and Bernhard Schölkopf, editors, *Advances in Neural Information Processing Systems 16*. MIT Press, Cambridge, MA, 2004.

K. Terzić, L. Hotz, and B. Neumann. Division of work during behaviour recognition - the SCENIC approach. In *Workshop on Behaviour Modelling and Interpretation, 30th German Conference on Artificial Intelligence*, Osnabrück, Germany, September 2007.

S. Tobies. *Complexity results and practical algorithms for logics in Knowledge Representation*. Phd thesis, LuFG Theoretical Computer Science, RWTH-Aachen, Germany, 2001.

D. Tsarkov and I. Horrocks. Fact++ description logic reasoner: System description. In *Proceedings of the International Joint Conference on Automated Reasoning (IJCAR)*, 2006. http://owl.man.ac.uk/factplusplus/.

W3C Recommendation. Owl web ontology language overview, 2004. URL http://www.w3.org/TR/owl-features/.

W3C Working Group Note. A semantic web primer for object-oriented software developers, 2006. URL http://www.w3.org/TR/sw-oosd-primer/.

T. Wagner, U. Visser, A. D. Lattner, and O. Herzog. Qualitative egocentric updating for autonomous mobiles. In *5th IFAC Symposium on Intelligent Autonomous Vehicles*, July 5 - 7 2004.

J. O. Wallgrün, L. Frommberger, D. Wolter, F. Dylla, and C. Freksa. Qualitative spatial representation and reasoning in the SparQ-toolbox. In *Spatial Cognition*, pages 39–58, 2006.

M. Wessel. Obstacles on the way to qualitative spatial reasoning with description logics: Some undecidability results. In *Description Logics*, 2001.

T. Winograd. Frame representations and the declarative/procedural contraversy. In R. Brachman and H. Levesque, editors, *Readings in Knowledge Representation*, pages 357–370. Morgan Kaufmann, 1985.

Z. Yang. Fahrbahngeometriemodellierung und Videobasierte Pfeilmarkierungserkennung. Master's thesis, Universität Karlsruhe, Institut für Mess- und Regelungstechnik, 2006.

Die VDM Verlagsservicegesellschaft sucht für wissenschaftliche Verlage abgeschlossene und herausragende

Dissertationen, Habilitationen, Diplomarbeiten, Master Theses, Magisterarbeiten usw.

für die kostenlose Publikation als Fachbuch.

Sie verfügen über eine Arbeit, die hohen inhaltlichen und formalen Ansprüchen genügt, und haben Interesse an einer honorarvergüteten Publikation?

Dann senden Sie bitte erste Informationen über sich und Ihre Arbeit per Email an *info@vdm-vsg.de*.

Sie erhalten kurzfristig unser Feedback!

VDM Verlagsservicegesellschaft mbH
Dudweiler Landstr. 99
D - 66123 Saarbrücken
www.vdm-vsg.de

Telefon +49 681 3720 174
Fax +49 681 3720 1749

Die VDM Verlagsservicegesellschaft mbH vertritt

Printed by Books on Demand GmbH, Norderstedt / Germany